ADVANCE PRAISE FOR

How to Be a Stoic

"This is a lucid, engaging, and persuasive book about what it means to pursue Stoic ideals in the here and now. Massimo Pigliucci's imaginary conversations with Epictetus carry the reader effortlessly along while grounding the discussion firmly in the ancient Stoic tradition—and in his own life experience. The result is a compelling picture of a Stoic way of life that is consistent with contemporary science and philosophy, and is both eminently ethical and down-to-earth practical. It will be inviting to Stoics and non-Stoics alike who are willing to reason together seriously about how (and why) to be a modern Stoic."

—Lawrence C. Becker, author of *A New Stoicism*

"If you want to learn the ways of Stoicism, and you're living in the twenty-first century, this should be one of the first books you read. Massimo has written a fine primer for the aspiring Marcus Aurelius."

—Donald J. Robertson, author of *The Philosophy of CBT and Stoicism and the Art of Happiness*

About the Author

Massimo Pigliucci is the K. D. Irani Professor of Philosophy at the City College of New York. He holds PhDs in genetics, evolutionary biology, and philosophy and has written for many publications, including the *New York Times* and the *Washington Post*. The author or editor of ten books, he lives in New York City. Massimo blogs at platofootnote.org and at howtobeastoic.org.

HOW TO BE A
STOIC

ANCIENT WISDOM

FOR

MODERN LIVING

MASSIMO PIGLIUCCI

LONDON · SYDNEY · AUCKLAND · JOHANNESBURG

1 3 5 7 9 10 8 6 4 2

Rider, an imprint of Ebury Publishing,
20 Vauxhall Bridge Road,
London SW1V 2SA

Rider is part of the Penguin Random House group of companies whose
addresses can be found at global.penguinrandomhouse.com

Penguin
Random House
UK

First published in Great Britain by Rider in 2017
Published in the United States by Basic Books, an imprint of Perseus Books,
LLC, a subsidiary of Hachette Book Group, Inc.

www.penguin.co.uk

A CIP catalogue record for this book is available from the British Library

ISBN 9781846045073

Printed and bound in Great Britain by Clays Ltd, St Ives PLC

Penguin Random House is committed to a
sustainable future for our business, our readers
and our planet. This book is made from Forest
Stewardship Council® certified paper.

To Caley Luna, who has just begun her own journey into philosophy. May it change her life for the better, as it has mine. To Corinna, who has encouraged me a great deal to become a better person through the practice of Stoicism.

CONTENTS

**PART III. THE DISCIPLINE OF ASSENT:
HOW TO REACT TO SITUATIONS**

CHAPTER I

THE UNSTRAIGHTFORWARD PATH

Midway upon the journey of our life
I found myself within a forest dark,
For the straightforward pathway had been lost.

—DANTE, *THE DIVINE COMEDY: INFERNO*, CANTO I

IN EVERY CULTURE WE KNOW OF, WHETHER IT BE SECULAR or religious, ethnically diverse or not, the question of how to live is central. How should we handle life's challenges and vicissitudes? How should we conduct ourselves in the world and treat others? And the ultimate question: how do we best prepare for the final test of our character, the moment when we die?

The numerous religions and philosophies that have been devised over human history to address these issues offer answers ranging from the mystical to the hyper-rational. Recently, even science has gotten into the business, with an onslaught of technical papers and popular books on happiness and how to achieve it, accompanied by the obligatory brain scans displaying "your brain on . . . " whatever it is that may increase or decrease your satisfaction with life.

Correspondingly, the tools to seek answers to existential questions vary as much as the approaches that have been used—from sacred texts to deep meditation, from philosophical arguments to scientific experiments.

The resulting panorama is truly astounding and reflects both the creativity of the human spirit and the urgency that we obviously attach to inquiries into meaning and purpose. You can embrace any of a large variety of options within the Judeo-Christian-Islamic religions, for instance; or choose one of a panoply of schools of Buddhism; or opt instead for Taoism, or Confucianism, among many others. If philosophy, rather than religion, is your cup of tea, then you can turn to existentialism, secular humanism, secular Buddhism, ethical culture, and so forth. Or you can arrive instead at the conclusion that there is no meaning—indeed, the very search for it is meaningless—and embrace a "happy" sort of nihilism (yes, there is such a thing).

For my part, I've become a Stoic. I do not mean that I have started keeping a stiff upper lip and suppressing my emotions. As much as I love the character of Mr. Spock (which *Star Trek* creator Gene Roddenberry purportedly modeled after his—naïve, as it turns out—understanding of Stoicism), these traits represent two of the most common misconceptions about what it means to be a Stoic. In reality, Stoicism is not about suppressing or hiding emotion—rather, it is about acknowledging our emotions, reflecting on what causes them, and redirecting them for our own good. It is also about keeping in mind what is and what is not under our control, focusing our efforts on the former and not wasting them on the latter. It is about practicing virtue and excellence and navigating the world to the best of our abilities, while being mindful of the moral dimension of all our actions. As I explain in this book, in practice Stoicism involves a dynamic combination of reflecting on theoretical precepts, reading inspirational texts, and engaging in meditation, mindfulness, and other spiritual exercises.

One of the key tenets of Stoicism is that we ought to recognize, and take seriously, the difference between what we can and cannot master. This distinction—also made by some Buddhist doctrines—is often taken to indicate a tendency of Stoics to withdraw from social engagement and public life, but a closer look at both Stoic writings and, more importantly, the lives of famous Stoics will dispel this impression: Stoicism was very much a philosophy of social engagement and encouraged love for all humankind and Nature as well. It is this apparently contradictory tension between the advice to focus on one's thoughts and the social dimension of Stoicism that drew me to it as a practice.

I arrived at Stoicism, not on my way to Damascus, but through a combination of cultural happenstance, life's vicissitudes, and deliberate philosophical choice. In retrospect, it seems inevitable that my path would eventually lead me to the Stoics. Raised in Rome, I have considered Stoicism part of my cultural heritage ever since I studied ancient Greek and Roman history and philosophy in high school, although it wasn't until recently that I sought to make its principles part of my everyday life.

I am by profession a scientist and philosopher, and I have therefore always been inclined to seek more coherent ways to understand the world (through science) and better choices for living my life (through philosophy). A few years ago, I wrote a book, *Answers for Aristotle: How Science and Philosophy Can Lead Us to a More Meaningful Life*, in which I explored such a framework, which I called *sciphi*. The basic approach was to combine the ancient idea of virtue ethics, which focuses on character development and the pursuit of personal excellence as the pillars providing meaning to our lives, with the latest that the natural and social sciences tell us about human nature and how we work, fail, and learn. As it happened, this was only the beginning of my journey toward philosophical self-awareness.

Something else was going on at the time that made me pause and reflect. I have not been a religious person since my teenage years (I was prompted to leave Catholicism, in part, by reading Bertrand Russell's famous *Why I Am Not a Christian* in high school), and as such I have been on my own in dealing with questions of where my morals and the meaning in my life come from. I take it that an increasing number of people in the United States and across the world find themselves facing a similar conundrum. While sympathetic to the idea that lack of religious affiliation should be just as acceptable a choice in life as any religious one, and strongly supportive of the constitutional separation of church and state in the United States and elsewhere, I have also grown increasingly dissatisfied with (make that downright irritated by) the intolerant anger of the so-called New Atheists, represented by Richard Dawkins and Sam Harris, among others. Although public criticism of religion (or of *any* idea) is the staple of a healthy democratic society, people don't respond very well to being belittled and insulted. On this point the

Stoic philosopher Epictetus clearly agrees with me, all the while displaying his characteristic sense of humor: "At this point you run the risk of him saying, 'What business is that of yours, sir? What are you to me?' Pester him further, and he is liable to punch you in the nose. I myself was once keen for this sort of discourse, until I met with just such a reception."

There are, of course, alternatives to the New Atheism if you want to pursue a nonreligious approach to life, including secular Buddhism and secular humanism. Yet these two paths—the two major ones on offer for those seeking a meaningful secular existence—are somehow unsatisfactory to me, though for opposite reasons. I find Buddhism's currently dominant modes a bit too mystical, and its texts opaque and hard to interpret, especially in light of what we know about the world and the human condition from modern science (and despite a number of neurobiological studies that persuasively show the mental benefits of meditation). Secular humanism, which I have embraced for years, suffers from the opposite problem: it is *too* dependent on science and a modern conception of rationality, with the result that—despite the best efforts of its supporters—it comes across as cold and not the sort of thing you want to bring your kids to on a Sunday morning. Hence, I think, the spectacular lack of success (numerically speaking) of secular humanist organizations.

By contrast, in Stoicism I have found a rational, science-friendly philosophy that includes a metaphysics with a spiritual dimension, is explicitly open to revision, and, most importantly, is eminently practical. The Stoics accepted the scientific principle of universal causality: everything has a cause, and everything in the universe unfolds according to natural processes. There is no room for spooky transcendental stuff. But they also believed that the universe is structured according to what they called the *Logos,* which can be interpreted as either God or simply what is sometimes termed "Einstein's god": the simple, indubitable fact that Nature is understandable by reason.

Although other components of the Stoic system are important, by far the distinguishing feature of Stoicism is its practicality: it began in the guise of, and has always been understood as, a quest for a happy and meaningful life. Not surprisingly, then, its fundamental texts—pretty much all of them coming to us from the late Roman Stoa (as the Stoic school was called), since most of the early writings have been lost—are paragons of clarity. Epictetus, Seneca, Musonius Rufus, and Marcus Aurelius speak to us in plain language, far removed from the often cryptic Buddhist texts or even the flowery allegories of early Christianity. One of my favorite quotations, again from Epictetus, exemplifies this down-to-earth practicality: "Death is necessary and cannot be avoided. I mean, where am I going to go to get away from it?"

The final reason I turned to Stoicism is that this philosophy speaks most directly and convincingly to the inevitability of death and how to prepare for it. I recently passed the half-century mark, a seemingly arbitrary point in life that nonetheless prompted me to engage in broader reflections: who am I, and what am I doing? As a nonreligious person, I was also looking for some sort of playbook on how to prepare for the eventual end of my life. Beyond my own preoccupations, we live in a society where life keeps being extended by modern science and more and more of us will consequently find ourselves needing to decide what to do with our existence for decades after retiring. Moreover, whatever we decide about the meaning of our extended lives, we also need to find ways of preparing ourselves and our loved ones to face the permanent demise of our own consciousness, of our unique presence in this world. And we need to know how to die in a dignified way that allows us to achieve tranquillity of mind and is of comfort to those who survive us.

Famously, the original Stoics devoted a great deal of effort and many writings to what Seneca referred to as the ultimate test of character and principle. "We die every day," he wrote to his friend Gaius Lucillius. Seneca connected this test to the rest of our existence on earth: "A man cannot live well if he knows not how to die well." Life, for the Stoics, is an ongoing project, and death, its logical, natural end point, is nothing special in and of itself and nothing that we should particularly fear. This view resonated with me, striking a balance as it did between opposite attitudes to which I had been exposed and which I found unpalatable: no fantasizing about an immortality of which there is neither evidence nor reason to believe in, but also no secular dismissal—or worse, avoidance—of the issue of death and personal extinction.

For these and other reasons, I'm not alone in my quest to revive this ancient practical philosophy and adapt it to twenty-first-century life. Every fall thousands of people participate in Stoic Week, a worldwide philosophy event-cum–social science experiment organized by a team at the University of Exeter in England, with the collaboration of academic philosophers, cognitive therapists, and everyday practitioners from all over the world. The goal of Stoic Week is twofold: on the one hand, to get people to learn about Stoicism and its relevance to their lives, and on the other hand, to collect systematic data to see whether practicing Stoicism actually makes a difference. The preliminary results from the Exeter initiative are tentative (in future Stoic Weeks, more sophisticated experimental protocols will be used and larger sample sizes collected), but they are promising. Participants in the third international Stoic Week, for instance, reported a 9 percent increase in positive emotions, an 11 percent decrease in negative emotions, and a 14 percent improvement in life satisfaction after one week of practice. (The previous year the team conducted longer-term follow-ups, and they confirmed the initial results for people who kept practicing.) Participants also seem to think that Stoicism makes them more virtuous: 56 percent gave Stoic practice a high mark in that regard. Of course, this is a self-selected sample of people who have an interest in Stoicism and buy into at least some of its assumptions and practices. Then again, for people who are already somewhat committed to this particular approach to see such significant changes in the span of a few days ought to at least encourage interested others to pay attention.

Results like these are not entirely surprising, given that Stoicism is the philosophical root of a number of evidence-based psychological therapies, including Viktor Frankl's logotherapy and Albert Ellis's rational emotive behavior therapy. Of Ellis it has been said that "no individual—not even Freud himself—has had a greater impact on modern psychotherapy." Frankl was a neurologist and psychiatrist who survived the Holocaust and wrote the best-selling book *Man's Search for Meaning.* His moving and inspiring story of resilience can be read as a contemporary example of Stoicism in practice. Both Ellis and Frankl acknowledged Stoicism as an important influence in developing their therapeutic approaches, with Frankl characterizing logotherapy as a type of existential analysis. Another compelling account of Stoicism is provided by Vice Admiral James Stockdale in his memoir *In Love and War.* Stockdale famously credited Stoicism (and in particular his readings of Epictetus) for his survival under prolonged horrid conditions in a Vietnamese prisoner-of-war camp. Also owing a significant debt to Stoicism is the increasingly diverse family of practices that goes under the general rubric of cognitive behavioral therapy (CBT), which was initially deployed to treat depression and now is more widely applied to a variety of mental conditions. Aaron T. Beck, author of *Cognitive Therapy of Depression,* acknowledges this debt when he writes, "The philosophical origins of cognitive therapy can be traced back to the Stoic philosophers."

Of course, Stoicism is a philosophy, not a type of therapy. The difference is crucial: a therapy is intended to be a short-term approach to helping people overcome specific problems of a psychological nature; it doesn't necessarily provide a general picture, or philosophy, of life. A philosophy of life is something we all need, however, and something we all develop, consciously or not. Some people simply import wholesale whatever framework for life they acquire from a religion. Others make up their own philosophy as they go along, without thinking too much about it, but nonetheless engaging in actions and decisions that reflect some implicit understanding of what life is about. Still others would rather—as Socrates famously put it—take the time to examine their life in order to live it better.

Stoicism, like any life philosophy, may not appeal to or work for everyone. It is rather demanding, stipulating that moral character is the only truly worthy thing to cultivate; health, education, and even wealth are considered "preferred indifferents" (although Stoics don't advocate asceticism, and many of them historically enjoyed the good things in life). Such "externals" do not define who we are as individuals and have nothing to do with our personal worth, which depends on our character and our exercise of the virtues. In this sense, Stoicism is eminently democratic, cutting across social classes: whether you are rich or poor, healthy or sick, educated or ignorant, it makes no difference to your ability to live a moral life and thus achieve what the Stoics called *ataraxia*, or tranquillity of mind.

For all its uniqueness, Stoicism has numerous points of contact with other philosophies, with religions (Buddhism, Taoism, Judaism, and Christianity), and with modern movements such as secular humanism and ethical culture. There is something very appealing to me, as a nonreligious person, in the idea of such an ecumenical philosophy, one that can share goals and at least some general attitudes with other major ethical traditions across the world. This commonality has allowed me to reject more forcefully the strident New Atheism that I criticized earlier, and it also allows religious persons to distance themselves from the even more pernicious fundamentalisms of different stripes that have been plaguing our recent history. To a Stoic, it ultimately does not matter if we think the Logos is God or Nature, as long as we recognize that a decent human life is about the cultivation of one's character and concern for other people (and even for Nature itself) and is best enjoyed by way of a proper—but not fanatical—detachment from mere worldly goods.

There are also, naturally, challenges that remain unresolved, and which I will explore along with the reader in *How to Be a Stoic*. The original Stoicism, for instance, was a comprehensive philosophy that included not only ethics but also a metaphysics, a natural science, and specific approaches to logic and epistemology (that is, a theory of knowledge). The Stoics considered these other aspects of their philosophy important because they fed into and informed their main concern: how to live one's life. The idea was that in order to decide on the best approach to living we also need to understand the nature of the world (metaphysics), how it works (natural science), and how (imperfectly) we come to understand it (epistemology).

But many of the particular notions developed by the ancient Stoics have ceded place to new ones introduced by modern science and philosophy and need therefore to be updated. For instance, as William Irvine explains in his lucid *A Guide to the Good Life*, the clear dichotomy the Stoics drew between what is and is not under our control is too strict: beyond our own thoughts and attitudes, there are some things that we can and, depending on circumstances, must influence—up to the point where we recognize that nothing more is in our power to be done. It is also true, conversely, that the Stoics turned out to be overly optimistic about how much control human beings have over their own thoughts. Modern cognitive science has shown over and over again that we are often prey to cognitive biases and delusions. But in my view, this knowledge reinforces the idea that we need to train ourselves in virtuous and right thinking, as the Stoics advised.

Finally, one of the most attractive features of Stoicism is that the Stoics were open to considering challenges to their doctrines and altering them accordingly. In other words, it is an open-ended philosophy, ready to incorporate criticism from other schools (for instance, the so-called Skeptics of ancient times) as well as new discoveries. As Seneca famously put it: "Men who have made these discoveries before us are not our masters, but our guides. Truth lies open for all; it has not yet been monopolized. And there is plenty of it left even for posterity to discover." In a world of fundamentalism and hardheaded doctrines, it is refreshing to embrace a worldview that is inherently open to revision.

For all these reasons, I have decided to commit to Stoicism as a philosophy of life, to explore it, to study it, to find areas of improvement if possible, and to share it with like-minded others. In the end, of course, Stoicism is yet another (unstraightforward) path devised by humanity to develop a more coherent view of the world, of who we are, and of how we fit into the broader scheme of things. The need for this sort of insight seems to be universal, and in *How to Be a Stoic* I will do my best to guide the reader down this ancient and yet remarkably modern road.

The problem is that I myself am rather a novice when it comes to Stoic philosophy, so we actually need to turn to a more expert chaperone, someone who can gently show us the way, nudging us away from the most common mistakes and keeping us on the path toward enlightenment. When Dante Alighieri went on his own spiritual journey—which resulted in the writing of the beautiful *Divine Comedy*—he imagined himself suddenly lost in the middle of a dark forest, with his way forward uncertain. It turned out that he was at the (imaginary) entrance to Hell, about to descend into its depths. Lucky for him, he had a sure mentor to guide him on his journey, the Roman poet Virgil. The journey we are about to embark upon is not as momentous as a visit to Hell, and this book certainly is no *Divine Comedy*, but in a sense we are lost too, and in need of guidance just as surely as Dante was. My choice for the role of our guide is Epictetus, the very first Stoic I encountered when I began my own exploration of that philosophy.

Epictetus was born in Hierapolis (present-day Pamukkale in Turkey) around the year 55 CE. Epictetus was not his real name, which is lost to us: the word simply means "acquired," reflecting the fact that he was a slave. His known master was Epaphroditos, a wealthy freedman (that is, a former slave himself) who worked as a secretary to the emperor Nero in Rome, which is where Epictetus spent his youth. He was crippled, either by birth or because of an injury received while he was a slave under a former master. At any rate, Epaphroditos treated Epictetus well and allowed him to study Stoic philosophy under one of the most renowned teachers in Rome, Musonius Rufus.

After Nero's death in 68 CE, Epictetus was freed by his master—a common practice in Rome with particularly intelligent and educated slaves. He then set up his own school in the capital of the empire, and taught there until 93 CE, when the emperor Domitian banned all philosophers from the city. (Philosophers in general, and Stoics in particular, were persecuted by a number of emperors, especially Vespasian and Domitian. Scores of philosophers were either killed—including Seneca right before the end of Nero's reign—or exiled, as happened twice to Musonius. The Stoic penchant for speaking truth to power, as we would say today, did not go over well with some of the people who held very dearly to that power.)

Epictetus then moved his school to Nicopolis in northwestern Greece, where he may have been visited by the emperor Hadrian (one of the five so-called good emperors, the last of whom was Marcus Aurelius, arguably the most famous Stoic of all time). Epictetus became renowned as a teacher and attracted a number of high-profile students, including Arrian of Nicomedia, who transcribed some of the master's lectures. Those lectures are known today as the *Discourses*, and I will use them as the basis for our exploration of Stoicism in this book. Epictetus never married, though late in his life he began to live with a woman who helped him raise the child of a friend, a boy who would have otherwise been left to die. Epictetus himself died around 135 CE.

What a remarkable figure, no? A crippled slave who acquires an education, becomes a free man, establishes his own school, is exiled by one emperor but is on friendly terms with another, and selflessly helps a young child near the end of a simple life that will continue until the very ripe age, especially for the time, of eighty. Oh, and most importantly, who utters some of the most powerful words ever spoken by any teacher in the entire Western world and beyond. Epictetus is the perfect guide for our journey, not simply because he was the first Stoic I happened to encounter, but because of his sensitivity and intelligence, his dark sense of humor, and his disagreement with me on a number of important points, which will allow me to demonstrate the remarkable flexibility of Stoic philosophy and its capacity to adapt to times and places as different from each other as second-century Rome and twenty-first-century New York.

So let us explore Stoicism together in a running conversation with Epictetus via his discourses. We will talk about subjects as varied as God, cosmopolitanism in an increasingly fractured world, taking care of our families, the relevance of our own character, managing anger and disability, the morality (or not) of suicide, and a lot more. Other Stoic authors, both ancient and modern, will occasionally supplement what we learn from Epictetus, and sometimes I will gently push back against some of our guide's notions, bringing up advances in philosophy and science over the intervening centuries and debating what a modern take on Stoicism might look like. The goal is to learn something about how to answer that most fundamental question: How ought we to live our lives?

CHAPTER 2

A ROAD MAP FOR THE JOURNEY

What is the goal of virtue, after all, except a life that flows
smoothly?

—EPICTETUS, *DISCOURSES*, I.4

WHEN I TRAVEL AROUND IN SOMEPLACE NEW, I LIKE TO
bring along a map of the territory. It gives me a sense of where
I'm going, where I shouldn't go, and a context for all the
things I will be experiencing during the journey. This chapter
is a map of the broad contours of Stoicism, as well as a summary of the guiding principles that structure the rest of the
book, so that you may make the most out of this experience.
I am convinced that we can hardly appreciate a philosophy or
a religion (or any complex idea, really) without some understanding of its often nonlinear path of development, and so
let's begin with a closer look at the history of the philosophy
that we are about to explore, and which you might decide to
apply to your life.

As the story is told by Diogenes Laertius in his *Lives of
the Eminent Philosophers*, Stoicism began in Athens, Greece,
around the year 300 BCE. Zeno, a Phoenician merchant and

native of Citium (modern-day Cyprus) who, we are assured, was fond of eating green figs and basking in the sun, became interested in philosophy after being shipwrecked on a voyage from Phoenicia to Peiraeus with a cargo of purple. He went up into Athens and sat down in a bookseller's shop, being then a man of thirty. As he went on reading the second book of Xenophon's Memorabilia, he was so pleased that he inquired where men like Socrates were to be found. Crates [a Cynic philosopher] passed by in the nick of time, so the bookseller pointed to him and said, "Follow yonder man."

Zeno did follow Crates and became his student. One of the first things he learned from his new teacher was to practice not being ashamed of things of which there is nothing to be ashamed. Crates had Zeno go around with a potful of lentil soup. Crates then broke the pot, and Zeno took to flight in shame, with his teacher yelling after him, in full view of a crowd: "Why run away, my little Phoenician? Nothing terrible has befallen you." Zeno studied under Crates and other philosophers for several years, after which he felt confident enough to start his own school. While initially his followers were, predictably enough, called Zenonians, eventually they began to be referred to as "Stoics," because they met under the Stoa Poikile, or painted porch, a public place in the center of the city. Anyone could come by and listen to Zeno talk about a number of topics, from human nature to duty, law, education, poetry, rhetoric, and ethics, among others. (We know this because, although few of Zeno's writings have survived, the titles of his books are listed by Diogenes Laertius.) Zeno died at a very old age (one source says he was ninety-eight), either of a fall or, having reckoned that he was in pain and could no longer be useful to society, by committing suicide by starvation.

After Cleanthes, Zeno's pupil and the second head of the Stoa, came another pivotal figure in the history of our philosophical movement: Chrysippus of Soli, who was a long-distance runner before he turned to philosophy. He wrote many books about all sorts of subjects (Diogenes Laertius mentions the incredible figure of 705!) and, more importantly, introduced a great number of new ideas—so many in fact that the ancients used to say that "but for Chrysippus, there had been no Porch."

Stoicism didn't come out of nowhere, of course. The early Stoics were heavily influenced by previous philosophical schools and thinkers, in particular by Socrates and by the Cynics, but also by the Academics (followers of Plato) (see the appendix for more on these different schools of thought). They spent a significant amount of time engaging rivals in lively debate, especially the Academics, the Peripatetics (followers of Aristotle), and of course the Epicureans. Epictetus, for instance, devotes three entire chapters of the *Discourses* to rebutting Epicurus. Each of these schools was "eudaimonic"—that is, their objective was to figure out the best way of living a human life. Some emphasized virtue (the Peripatetics, the Cynics, and the Stoics), and others pleasure (the Epicureans, the Cyrenaics) while still others were more interested in metaphysics (the Academics) or in the limits of human knowledge (the Skeptics). All, however, aimed at the same goal: a flourishing existence.

This went on for a while, until in 155 BCE something very important happened to ancient philosophy: the heads of the

Stoa (Diogenes of Babylon), the Academy, and the Peripatetic school were chosen as ambassadors to represent Athens in political negotiations with Rome. The philosophers went to the capital of the Republic to plead for the reduction of a fine that had been imposed three years earlier on Athens for the sack of Oropus, a small Greek city under Roman protection. The Athenians' visit had a great cultural impact, far beyond its diplomatic import: the philosophers gave packed lectures in the capital, shocking the rather conservative Roman establishment and igniting an interest in philosophy among the Romans for the first time.

Then, during the years 88–86 BCE, two philosophers, the Peripatetic Athenion and the Epicurean Aristion, briefly in turn gained absolute power in Athens. (Imagine that: a philosopher turned dictator!) However, they made the strategically fatal mistake of siding with King Mithridates against the Romans, an alliance that eventually led to the sack of Athens. The episode spelled the end of that venerable city as the philosophical capital of the ancient world, as major exponents of all schools moved to quieter places, including Rhodes, Alexandria, and especially Rome itself. It was a pivotal moment in the history of Western philosophy.

This transitional, second period of Stoic history is referred to as the "middle Stoa." The great Roman orator Cicero, who was sympathetic to Stoic ideas, is one of our major sources for both the early and the middle Stoa. Eventually, the Roman Republic—after the death of Julius Caesar and the ascent to power of Octavian Augustus—gave way to the Empire. Stoicism thrived as a major school during this time, known as the "late Stoa." Active then were all the famous Stoics whose writings have been preserved in sizable quantities: Gaius Musonius Rufus (Epictetus's teacher), Seneca (the adviser to the emperor Nero), Epictetus himself, and the emperor-philosopher Marcus Aurelius.

By the time Emperor Constantine legalized Christianity in 312 CE, Stoicism was in decline, as were a number of other schools of thought. Eventually, the Byzantine emperor Justinian closed the Academy in 529 CE, thus ending the ancient Greco-Roman philosophical tradition altogether. The idea of Stoicism, however, survived in the writings of the many historical figures who were influenced by it (including those who were sometimes critical of it), among them some of the Early Church Fathers, Augustine, Boethius, Thomas Aquinas, Giordano Bruno, Thomas More, Erasmus, Montaigne, Francis Bacon, Descartes, Montesquieu, and Spinoza. Modern Existentialism and even neo-orthodox Protestant theology have also been influenced by Stoicism. In the twentieth century, Stoicism saw a resurgence after the Second World War, when, as we have seen, it inspired Viktor Frankl's logotherapy, Albert Ellis's rational emotive behavior therapy, and the broad family of cognitive behavioral therapies.

Although Stoicism was designed from the beginning as a very practical philosophy, it would not be a "philosophy" if it were not based on a theoretical framework of some sort. That framework is the idea that in order to live a good (in the sense of eudaimonic) life, one has to understand two things: the nature of the world (and by extension, one's place in it) and the nature of human reasoning (including when it fails, as it so often does).

An ancient student of Stoicism would probably have pursued these goals by studying physics, logic, and ethics, although each of those terms meant something a bit different from what we mean by them today. Stoic "physics" was the study of how the world works, and it included what we today call the natural sciences, plus metaphysics (nowadays a branch of philosophy) and even theology. (The Stoics believed in God, though theirs was a material God immanent in the cosmos.) Stoic "logic" included what we today call by that name—that is, the study of formal reasoning, to which the ancient Stoics in fact made fundamental contributions. But it also encompassed modern epistemology (that is, a theory of knowledge), rhetoric (the study of how to best convey ideas to others), and psychology (in particular an understanding of how the human mind works and how and when it fails to reason properly).

The Stoics didn't study physics and logic for their own sake. Like Socrates before them—and unlike a number of other philosophers then and since—they were not interested in theory for theory's sake. If philosophy was not useful to human life, then it wasn't useful at all. But how exactly were physics and logic connected to the goal of living the good life, which was the proper object of study of Stoic ethics? It is illuminating to realize where our words "ethics" and "morality" come from in the first place. "Ethics" derives from the Greek *êthos*, a word related to our idea of character; "morality" comes from the Latin *moralis*, which has to do with habits and customs. Indeed, *moralis* is how Cicero translated the Greek word *êthos*! So the basic idea is that a good character cannot be properly developed, and good habits practiced, without an understanding of the other two areas of inquiry.

The Stoics used several metaphors to get their point across. One of the most incisive is that of a garden, introduced by Chrysippus, who said that the fruits of the garden represent the ethics. To get good fruits we must nurture the plants with fine nutrients: the soil of the garden, then, is the physics, providing our understanding of the world in which we live. Moreover, our "garden" needs to be fenced off from unwanted and destructive influences, or it will be taken over by weeds and nothing good will grow in it: the fence is the logic, keeping bad reasoning out of the way.

Our friend Epictetus developed his own highly original take on why the three Stoic areas of study are important:

> There are three departments in which a man who is to be good and noble must be trained. The first concerns the will to get and will to avoid; he must be trained not to fail to get what he wills to get nor fall into what he wills to avoid. The second is concerned with impulse to act and not to act, and, in a word, the sphere of what is fitting: that we should act in order, with due consideration, and with proper care. The object of the third is that we may not be deceived, and may not judge at random, and generally it is concerned with assent.

These are often referred to as the three Stoic disciplines: desire, action, and assent. They are directly related to the three areas of study—as well as to the four virtues (discussed in detail later)—in this way:

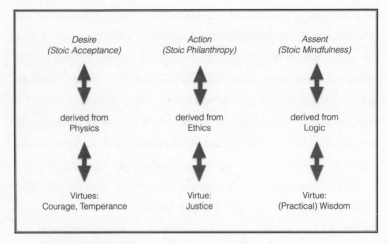

FIGURE 2.1. The relationships among the three Stoic disciplines (desire, action, and assent), the three areas of inquiry (physics, ethics, and logic), and the four cardinal virtues (courage, temperance, justice, and practical wisdom).

This diagram encapsulates a lot of Stoic thought, and mastering it is an excellent way to understand what the Stoics were after. The *discipline of desire* (also referred to as *Stoic acceptance*) tells us what is and is not proper to want. This, in turn, derives from the fact that some things are in our power and others are not. We can appreciate that crucial difference from an understanding of how the world works, as only people who are not schooled in physics make the mistake of thinking that they control more than they actually do (that is, they engage in wishful thinking). Two of the four Stoic virtues are pertinent to regulating desire: courage (to face facts and act accordingly) and temperance (to rein in our desires and make them commensurate with what is achievable). The *discipline of action* (known also as *Stoic philanthropy*, in the sense of concern for others) tells us how to behave in the world. It is the result of a proper understanding of ethics, the study of how to live our lives, and it draws on the virtue of justice. Finally, the *discipline of assent* (or *Stoic mindfulness*) tells us how to react to situations, in the sense of either giving our assent to our initial impressions of a situation or withdrawing it. This discipline is arrived at via the study of logic—what is and is not reasonable to think—and requires the virtue of practical wisdom.

This book is organized around the three disciplines. We will begin with desire—what is and is not proper to want—by studying the fundamental Stoic distinction between what is and what is not in our power, a distinction that in turn provides us with a useful framework for guidance in all our major life decisions. We'll come to appreciate why the Stoics said that we should "follow nature," that is, understand human nature and our place in the cosmos; play ball (metaphorically speaking) with Socrates to aid our good living by putting external goods (health, wealth, education), or their lack, in the proper perspective; and examine the Stoic take on God and purpose in the universe.

The second part of the book is devoted to the exploration of the discipline of action, or how to behave in the world. We will see why the Stoics thought that character is what matters the most, regardless of our circumstances; why they held that people don't really do evil but simply have misguided views of the world that sometimes lead them to do awful things; why they considered role models to be crucial for our education and inspiration, and how to choose good ones; and how Stoicism can help people in very challenging situations, including severe physical disability and mental illness.

The third section will tackle the discipline of assent, or how to best react to situations. This discipline comes into play with a wide variety of everyday problems, such as anger, anxiety, and loneliness, but also in positive aspects of our lives, like friendship and love. We shall see how the Stoics prepared themselves for the inevitable demise at the end of life and explore their sophisticated and nuanced thinking about the delicate issue of suicide. Finally, I will guide you through twelve selected spiritual exercises to get you started on your way to becoming a good student of Stoicism and as good a person as you can be.

PART I

THE DISCIPLINE OF DESIRE:
WHAT IT IS PROPER TO WANT
OR NOT TO WANT

CHAPTER 3

SOME THINGS ARE IN OUR POWER, OTHERS ARE NOT

We must make the best of those things that are in our power, and take the rest as nature gives it.

—EPICTETUS, *DISCOURSES*, I.1

I CAME TO THE UNITED STATES BACK IN 1990. I KNEW LITtle of American culture—other than what could be gleaned growing up watching Hollywood movies and television series dubbed in Italian—and a close friend suggested that I start my informal education by reading a short novel by Kurt Vonnegut.

Slaughterhouse-Five, published in 1969, is a strange work. The protagonist, Billy Pilgrim, finds himself abducted by an alien race known as the Tralfamadorians (or so he thinks), who put him in a zoo together with another captured earthling, the porn star Montana Wildhack. The Tralfamadorians are capable of moving in four dimensions—the standard three in space, plus time—and so can revisit any moment of their lives as they wish. Billy picks up this trick from his captors and then uses it to narrate crucial moments in his life, including the controversial Allied bombing of Dresden near the end of World War II.

It was while reading *Slaughterhouse-Five* that I first encountered these words, which are framed in Billy's optometry office on Earth and also inscribed in a locket worn by Montana:

> *God, grant me the serenity to accept the things I cannot change,*
> *Courage to change the things I can,*
> *And wisdom to know the difference.*

This, of course, is the Serenity Prayer, which encapsulates our hero's quest throughout the book: Billy very much wants serenity, and he thinks he can achieve it by recognizing that the past cannot be changed, that he can only affect the here and now. This recognition takes courage—not the kind needed in battle, but the more subtle, and yet arguably more important, kind needed to live your life to your best.

The prayer in its modern form is attributed to Reinhold Niebuhr, an American theologian who used it in his sermons as early as 1934. Today it's best known because of its use in the meetings of Alcoholics Anonymous and a number of other twelve-step organizations. The same sentiment is detectable, however, across centuries and cultures. Solomon ibn Gabirol, an eleventh-century Jewish philosopher, expressed it this way: "And they said: At the head of all understanding—is realizing what is and what cannot be, and the consoling of what is not in our power to change." Shantideva, an eighth-century Buddhist scholar, similarly wrote: "If there's a remedy when trouble strikes / What reason is there for dejection? / And if there is no help for it / What use is there in being glum?"

Yet there is an even more ancient version: "Make the best use of what is in your power, and take the rest as it happens. Some things are up to us and some things are not up to us. Our opinions are up to us, and our impulses, desires, aversions—in short, whatever is our own doing. Our bodies are not up to us, nor are our possessions, our reputations, or our public offices, or, that is, whatever is not our own doing." That one is found in Epictetus's *Enchiridion* (or *Handbook*), right at the beginning. Because this idea is foundational to Epictetus's teachings, and crucial to the whole system of Stoic philosophy going back to Zeno, we begin our exploration of Stoicism by considering it in some detail.

The parallels between these teachings hint that the influence of Stoic wisdom has been widespread, if often unrecognized, for many centuries. Moreover, some of the key concepts of Stoicism are found in other philosophical and religious traditions, including Judaism, Christianity, Buddhism, and Taoism. Some of these parallels are the result of direct or indirect reciprocal influence, and others represent the independent convergence of wise minds reflecting on the human condition. Although this book is concerned primarily with Stoicism, we will repeatedly encounter ideas that have been proposed, rediscovered, and validated through practice by people living in very different times and cultures. Since these are ideas that have truly withstood the test of time, we would be wise to draw from them in our own lives.

One day not so long ago, having recently reread Vonnegut's novel, I was walking in the Roman Forum and thinking about the words of my wise friend Epictetus when it occurred to me that there was a problem: he was both conceding too much and not enough. Epictetus lists our opinions, impulses, desires, and aversions as "up to us," and the condition of our bodies, possessions, and reputations and the public offices we hold as *not* up to us. That can't be right, I told him. On the one hand, my opinions are influenced by other people through what I read, or hear, or discuss. As for my impulses, desires, and aversions, many of them seem to spring up naturally and instinctively, and all I have available is some veto power when it comes to translating a thought into action. (Confirming my thought, I was distracted at that very moment by some gorgeous-looking gelato in a shop window, but I didn't need it, and it wouldn't have been good for my waistline, so I refrained from getting it.) On the other hand, I can certainly take care of my body by, say, going to the gym and eating healthy food; I can decide what to acquire, within my financial limits; and my reputation is also something I can work on, with colleagues, students, friends, and family. Moreover, even though I do not hold public office, the decision would certainly be mine if I were to seek it, as would my efforts to put myself forth as a candidate and work on a campaign to gather votes.

I was in the midst of articulating all this to my Stoic master when I suddenly realized that my twenty-first-century smugness had caught up with me. *Of course* Epictetus knew all this. He was no intellectual slouch. He must have meant something different from the literal reading of his words. I'm not sure why this surprised me, since all texts need to be interpreted against some background information. One needs guidance to provide some context, and luckily I had the best one available right next to me during my walk in the Forum. I asked him: "How do you make sense of my objection?"

Epictetus's answer came, as it often does, by way of an analogy: "We act very much as if we were on a voyage. What can I do? I can choose out the helmsman, the sailors, the day, the moment. Then a storm arises. What do I care? I have fulfilled my task: another has now to act, the helmsman. If the weather is bad for sailing, we sit distracted and keep looking continually and ask, 'What wind is blowing?' 'The north wind.' What have we to do with that? 'When will the west wind blow?' When it so chooses, good sir."

As is clear from Epictetus's example, the so-called Stoic dichotomy of control—some things are up to us, other things are not—is really a recognition of *three* levels of influence that we have over the world. To begin with, we make certain choices, selecting some goals (the sea voyage) and what appear to us to be the best means to obtain them (the experienced sailors). Next, we need to recognize that it does not follow from just having made a choice that we can implement a given course of action. Our preferred helmsman, for instance, may be sick on that day, or his services may be too expensive for us. Finally, some factors are entirely out of our control and we cannot even begin to influence them, like the direction and intensity of the winds.

As it happens, I experienced a harrowingly concrete case of Epictetus's analogy while writing this book. With one of my brothers, I flew from Rome to London to a festival of music and philosophy. A lot about that trip was under our control: our agreement to go, and our acceptance of the organizers' choice of airline (which supplied a specific plane and "helmsman"). What was entirely outside of our control was what happened as we were about to land at Gatwick

Airport. We were close enough to the ground to distinctly see the landing strip when suddenly the plane's powerful engines roared and we felt a strong acceleration: the Airbus had abruptly halted its descent and was rapidly gaining altitude again. This was not a good sign, but the pilot played it cool. He came on the speaker system and told us that, because of "a traffic issue," we were going to turn around and resume the landing procedure. That turned out to be a euphemism for "almost landing on top of a plane that was still on the runway we were supposed to use," apparently unnoticed by the control tower! Only the prompt reflexes of the pilot and the Airbus's powerful engines had saved our lives—neither of which factors, obviously, we had any means to affect. I only knew what was happening because my neighbor, sitting by the window, told me what was unfolding in real time. Yet throughout this incident I felt strangely calm. I'd often wondered when something dangerous would happen during my travels. "When it so chooses, good sir." The old philosopher was right again.

One of Epictetus's crucial points is that we have a strange tendency to worry about, and concentrate our energies on, precisely those things we cannot control. On the contrary, the Stoics say, we should pay attention to the parameters in life's equation that we do control or influence: making sure that we have embarked on a voyage we really want to make, and for good reasons; spending some time researching the best crew (airline) for our ship (plane); and making related preparations. One of the first lessons from Stoicism, then, is to focus our attention and efforts where we have the most power and then let the universe run as it will. This will save us both a lot of energy and a lot of worry.

Another Stoic metaphor, from Cicero, may help illustrate the point. Consider an archer trying to hit a target. Cicero explains that the archer has a number of things under his control: he has decided how much to train and how intensely, he has chosen a bow and an arrow as a function of the distance and type of target, he has aimed as best as he can, and he has chosen the exact moment when to let the arrow go. In other words, if he has been a conscientious archer, he has done his best up to the moment when the arrow leaves his bow. Now the question is: will the arrow hit the target? That, very clearly, is not up to him.

After all, a sudden gust of wind could alter the course of the arrow, which would then miss the target altogether. Or something else might unexpectedly interpose itself between the archer and the target, say, a carriage passing by. Finally, the target itself might move away to avoid the flying weapon—especially if the target is an enemy soldier. That is why Cicero concluded that "the actual hitting of the mark [is] to be chosen but not to be desired," a superficially cryptic statement whose meaning should by now be fairly clear: the Stoic archer has deliberately chosen to *attempt* to hit the mark, and he has done the best he can do within his power to accomplish the goal. But he is also ready to accept a possible negative outcome with equanimity, because the outcome was never entirely under his control. Other variables entered into it—just as happens in pretty much anything we decide to do.

It was at this point during our conversation that I realized that what Epictetus was telling me had countless applications to my own life. Consider, for instance, the degree of "control" we have over our own bodies. Ever since I was little, I have struggled with my weight. I was a chubby kid and predictably the subject of much teasing at school. I later developed into a somewhat insecure teenager, particularly when it came to personal relationships, and especially with girls. I've gotten better over time, but the weight issue is still with me, and always will be. Yet a Stoic perspective is very helpful here. To begin with, I had no control over either my genetic makeup (the result of a random encounter of one of my father's sperm with one of my mother's eggs) or, just as crucially, my early developmental environment. I ate whatever my grandparents (with whom I grew up) gave me, in whatever quantities and at whatever frequencies they deemed appropriate. As a biologist specializing precisely in the study of nature versus nurture, I cannot stress enough just how much our habits are shaped by the early interaction between our genes and the environment of our infancy and childhood.

But this is no reason to give in to fatalism and helplessness. A critical part of growing up and maturing as an adult is asserting more control over one's life, including choices concerning what to eat and how much, whether to exercise and how diligently, and so forth. Thus, probably later than would have been ideal but nonetheless with determination, I began exercising moderately more than fifteen years ago, to maintain muscle tone and aerobic capacity. At approximately the same time, I also started reading about the basics of nutrition, paying attention to food labels, and generally trying to eat well and in moderation. I probably still slip in these habits more often than I'd like to admit, but their results have been clearly on the positive side: I am healthier and I look better, which in turn helps me feel psychologically better. But I still do not have—and will never have—the kind of slim and muscular body that for others is a natural gift, or that they are able to achieve through their own strenuous efforts (facilitated by their genetics and early development, of course). This used to be a nagging problem and source of frustration for me. No more. I now have internalized the Stoic attitude that I have control over some things (what I eat, whether to exercise), but not others (my genes, my early experiences, and a number of other external factors, including the efficacy of my exercise regime). So the outcome—the body that I have, the degree of health that I enjoy—is to be accepted with equanimity; it is "chosen, but not desired," as Cicero put it. I derive satisfaction from knowing that, quite irrespective of the actual outcome, I'm doing my best.

The Stoic dichotomy of control applies throughout our lives. Let's say you are up for a promotion at your job. You think it is reasonable that you will get it, given how many years you have been with the company, the quality of your performance reviews, and your good relationships with your coworkers and your boss. Suppose you are going to find out tomorrow whether you got the promotion or not. Adopting a Stoic approach will allow you to have a night of peaceful sleep beforehand and be ready in the morning to face whatever outcome comes your way, not with resignation but with confidence. Your confidence lies not in the outcome, however, for that is outside of your control. The outcome depends on too many variables, including the internal politics of your company, your boss's personal sympathy (or not) toward you, and how much competition you may have from colleagues. No, your confidence lies in knowing that you did whatever was in your power to do, because *that,* and only that, is under your control. The universe doesn't bow to your wishes, it does what it does; your boss, your co-workers, the shareholders of your company, your customers, and a number of other factors are part of the universe, so why would you expect them to do your bidding?

Or imagine you are a parent with a teenage daughter who has suddenly turned against you, despite a happy childhood and what you thought was a wonderful relationship. The normal reaction might be regret, for perhaps not having done everything possible when your daughter was younger, despite the fact that you can't really think of what else you might have done. You also feel powerless to control the situation and frustrated by your previously happy child simply not responding to you anymore, even seeming (at least momentarily) to despise you. Epictetus tells us that regret is a waste of our emotional energy. We cannot change the past—it is outside of our control. We can, and should, learn from it, but the only situations we can do something about are those happening here and now. The right attitude is to derive comfort from the knowledge that you did your best in raising your daughter—indeed, that you are still doing your best to help her through this difficult moment in her life. Whether you succeed or not, your levelheaded acceptance of the outcome will be best.

Notice that I am not counseling resignation. Stoicism is too often misinterpreted as a passive philosophy, yet resignation goes precisely against not just what the Stoics themselves said but also, more importantly, what they practiced. The Stoics we know of were teachers, politicians, generals, and emperors—hardly the sort of people who would have fallen into a fatalistic torpor. Rather, they were wise enough to make the distinction between their internal goals, over which they had control, and the external outcome, which they could influence but not control. As the Serenity Prayer says, it is the hallmark of a mature and wise person to realize that difference.

I keep another famous story of Stoic equanimity in mind whenever I find myself in difficult circumstances—which, luckily for me, are usually far less challenging than those faced by the protagonist of the story. Paconius Agrippinus was a first-century Stoic whose father had been put to death by the emperor Tiberius, allegedly for treason. In the year 67 CE, Agrippinus faced the same accusation (probably also unjustified) from another emperor, Nero. Epictetus recounts what unfolded: "News was brought him, 'Your trial is on in the Senate!' 'Good luck to it, but the fifth hour is come'—this was the hour when he used to take his exercise and have a cold bath—'let us go and take exercise.' When he had taken his exercise they came and told him, 'You are condemned.' 'Exile or death?' he asked. 'Exile.' 'And my property?' 'It is not confiscated.' 'Well then, let us go to Aricia and dine.'" Agrippinus's reaction may sound cocky, the sort of thing an unflappable hero in a Hollywood movie (perhaps played by Cary Grant, or Harrison Ford) might say, but unlikely to ever be uttered by an actual human being. And yet this is precisely the power of Stoicism: the internalization of the basic truth that we can control our behaviors but not their outcomes—let alone the outcomes of other people's behaviors—leads to the calm acceptance of whatever happens, secure in the knowledge that we have done our best given the circumstances.

Incidentally, a friend of Agrippinus's, the senator (and Stoic) Publius Clodius Thrasea Paetus, was also accused by

Nero's sycophants and was not so lucky. He was given the *liberum mortis arbitrium*, a free choice of death, as the Romans euphemistically put it: he was ordered to commit suicide. Accordingly, he turned to his dining companions and calmly excused himself, retired to his bedroom, and invited the quaestor who had brought the emperor's order to witness while he slit his veins. He then awaited his death while conversing with his friend Demetrius, a philosopher of the rival school of the Cynics, about the nature of the soul.

Agrippinus and Thrasea were obviously rather exceptional human beings, and thankfully many of us don't live under the rule of a capricious tyrant—though unfortunately, such leaders are still surprisingly common two millennia after Nero. What is important is the basic idea of the dichotomy of control and its implications. If we take this notion seriously, it turns out that most things are not really under our control, from small and insignificant matters to really important ones. The logical consequence of this realization—which is also endorsed by Buddhism and other philosophical and religious traditions—should be to practice non-attachment to things and people. This is a tricky idea, and another source of common misconceptions about Stoicism. Here is how Epictetus rather bluntly explained it to me (I later realized that he meant to momentarily stun me in order to allow my mind to open up a bit and entertain a notion that had been alien up to that point):

> What then is the proper training for this? In the first place, the principal and most important thing, on the very threshold so to speak, is that when you are attached to a thing, not a thing which cannot be taken away but

anything like a water jug, or a crystal cup, you should bear in mind what it is, that you may not be disturbed when it is broken. So should it be with persons; if you kiss your child, or brother, or friend . . . you must remind yourself that you love a mortal, and that nothing that you love is your very own; it is given you for the moment, not for ever nor inseparably, but like a fig or a bunch of grapes at the appointed season of the year, and if you long for it in winter you are a fool. So too if you long for your son or your friend, when it is not given you to have him, know that you are longing for a fig in winter time.

Pause for a minute and reread that passage before continuing. Like most people, I'm sure you can go along with what Epictetus says about attachment when he is talking about jugs and crystal cups—sure, of course there is no need to get attached to objects (even though a lot of us actually are!). After all, it is just a cup (or an iPhone), and it's no big deal if it breaks, even if it is an expensive cup (there is no such thing as an inexpensive iPhone). But a good number of us recoil in horror when the philosopher shifts his discourse to our own child, brother, or friend. How inhuman, you might say, to advise people not to care about their loved ones! What sort of sociopath could possibly make an analogy between my brother and a fig, whether in or out of season?

And yet, once I had time to reflect on it for a moment, I saw that Epictetus was not counseling me not to care for my loved ones, and moreover, that he was saying something true, as hard as it may be to swallow. Stoicism originated and thrived in times of political instability; people's lives could be upturned at a moment's notice, and death could befall any-one, at any age. Even Emperor Marcus Aurelius, who lived at the apogee of Roman power in the century following Epic-tetus and was strongly influenced by the Greek philosopher, had his share of misfortune. Of his thirteen children, only one son and four daughters outlived their father. And this was a family that had by far the most material comforts, the best food, and the highest-quality medical care the age could afford. (Marcus's personal physician was Galen, one of the most famous doctors of antiquity.)

More to the point, as we have already seen, Epictetus himself adopted a friend's son, saving the boy from what oth-erwise would have been certain death. So the philosopher clearly had compassion for other people and cared for them, even some not related to him by blood. What Epictetus was telling me, then, was that it is best to look the reality of life straight in the face, with courage. And that reality includes the fact that no one is immortal, no one is "ours" in the sense that we are entitled to him or her. Understanding this is not just a way to maintain sanity when a loved one dies, or a dear friend leaves for another country. (Exile was common then, just as moving for economic reasons or to escape violence and turmoil is now.) Facing this reality also reminds us to enjoy the company and love of our fellow humans as much as pos-sible while we can, trying hard not to take them for granted, because it is certain that one day we and they will be gone and the only right "season" for appreciating them will have passed. We always live *hic et nunc*—here and now.

The truth of this reality was bluntly shown to me by Fate this past summer, when I spent three days in Istanbul despite the misgivings of some family members, who had pointed out that the city was the site of a terrible terrorist attack just days before I was to arrive in the country. But I reckoned—correctly, as it turned out—that the likelihood of another attack so soon after that one, especially with the predictably heightened security in the aftermath, would make for an acceptably low risk. What I did not take into account, however, was the possibility of political upheaval.

One evening I was having dinner with a few friends at a wonderful Cretan restaurant in the historic district of Istanbul when I noticed that everyone at a nearby table, one of the few still occupied so late, was staring intensely into their phones. My immediate interpretation was that I was witnessing yet another example of the damaging effect of modern technology: a preference for checking Facebook over talking to dinner companions. But it soon became clear that I should have denied assent (as the Stoics would say) to that first impression, since these fellow diners were both too engrossed and too visibly concerned for that explanation to be correct. As it turned out, they were following the news that a coup was under way. The reaction at our table was remarkably calm as we finished the wine and kept chatting. My Turkish friends related the history of such events in their country and described the increasingly authoritarian and strongly pro-Islamic government of Prime Minister Recep Tayyip Erdoğan.

At some point we had to decide what to do. There were rumors that all bridges had been closed by the military; if true, that would have meant there was no way for us to cross back to our hotel in central Istanbul. As it turned out, only the two bridges on the Bosphorus, connecting the Asian and

European sides, were closed. So after failing to find a cab, we cautiously approached the bridge on foot. We saw police cars blocking some streets and curious people hanging around, wondering what to do. The good news was that social media networks were still up (they never went down, in fact), so we could reassure our families that we were okay, for now.

Indeed, the situation was eerily calm; people fished from the bridge while smoking cigarettes, as they would have done any other night. Puzzled, we reached our hotel and retired for the night. Over the next several hours we heard helicopters and fighter jets overhead, accompanied at one point by two loud explosions that turned out to come from nearby Taksim Square. But when we woke up in the morning, all appeared to be almost normal, with people in the streets (though not as many as usual) and coffee shops open (though not many museums). The airport hadn't reopened yet, so we kept a low profile, walking the neighborhood and just reading and keeping an eye on the news until we were told that our flight had been changed but was still scheduled to depart. We would be making our way to the airport around midnight, headed for Paris and then New York.

And here is where things got a bit more troubling. When we approached the airport in a taxi, the streets were blocked by hundreds of people cheering the failure of the coup, even though the whole thing had left thousands dead or injured, mostly in the capital of Ankara and some smaller cities throughout the country. As a general rule, it is not a good idea to be blocked in traffic in the midst of a frenzied crowd, especially when you don't speak the language. It's even more of a dispreferred indifferent when such a crowd is made up of mostly young men roused by blood that has been shed in their own streets. And you definitely don't want to see your taxi driver starting to shout at another driver out of frustration at not being able to move forward. In spite of these hazards, we eventually made it to the terminal, checked in, and safely flew to Europe and then to the United States.

To a student of Stoicism, the experience was first and foremost a strong reminder of the fundamental principle of this chapter: few things are under our control. I repeat that principle to myself every day and try to keep it constantly in mind, but there is nothing like a sudden overturn of the social order to forcefully bring the point home. Second, I was surprised at how calmly my companions and I behaved throughout those twenty-four hours in Istanbul. True, we were never in any apparent physical danger, but the situation was uncertain, and especially once we heard explosions and military planes overhead a bit of anxiety would not have been entirely out of place. Third, while driving through the chanting crowd at the airport, I was reminded of just how easy it is to manipulate people emotionally, playing on their fears and anger. It reinforced for me the Stoic idea that such emotions should never be given assent, but always kept in check in favor of developing more positive attitudes—such as, in this case, by trying to rationally understand why events were unfolding as they were and where the country was headed as a consequence. In Istanbul, the practice of Stoicism served me well under very unusual circumstances, reinforcing the idea that other people could benefit from it as well—even if they don't find themselves in the midst of a coup d'état.

Chapter 4

Living According to Nature

Is our other statement then incredible—that man's nature is civilized and affectionate and trustworthy?

—Epictetus, *Discourses*, IV.1

The Stoics were famous in antiquity for inventing a lot of new words in order to explain their philosophy to others, and also for being fond of short, pithy phrases to remind themselves of their basic tenets whenever the need arose. One such catchphrase, uttered in some form as early as Zeno of Citium, is that we should live our lives "according to nature."

What? I mockingly questioned Epictetus. Is Stoicism all of a sudden turning out to be some sort of tree-hugging new-age thing? No, he calmly assured me: "It is no ordinary task merely to fulfill man's promise. For what is Man? A rational animal, subject to death. At once we ask, from what does the rational element distinguish us? From wild beasts. And from what else? From sheep and the like. Look to it then that you do nothing like a wild beast, else you destroy the Man in you and fail to fulfill his promise."

That human beings are special in the animal world was perfectly clear to the ancients. Aristotle, for one, famously said that we are the rational animal—meaning not that we always behave rationally, since even cursory observation proves that not to be the case, but rather that we are *capable* of rationality. He also thought that we are political animals, meaning not that we engage in political campaigns or discourse (although of course we do that as well), but that we live and, more importantly, thrive in a *polis*—a community of other human beings. From Aristotle's insight that we are by nature both social and reasoning, the Stoics derived the notion that human life is about the application of reason to social living. The difference between Aristotle and the Stoics may seem subtle, but it is crucial: Aristotle thought that contemplation is the highest *purpose* of human life, because our unique *function* in the animal world is our ability to think. As you might imagine, this purpose might make for a rather insular existence, so the Stoics shifted the emphasis very much toward the social, essentially arguing that the point of life for human beings is to use reason to build the best society that it is humanly possible to build.

The problem these days is that the very idea of a human nature is now somewhat in trouble. Both scientists and philosophers are increasingly uncomfortable with the notion, and some reject it outright as the vestige of a parochial worldview. Yet I think they are seriously mistaken in doing so.

Up until the mid-nineteenth century, people in the West thought that animals, including humans, had been specially created, one by one, by an all-powerful God. From this view, they didn't have much trouble accepting what Aristotle was saying on the matter, reinterpreted through the filter of their particular religion: humanity is special because it is built in the image of God, and it has a built-in purpose—carrying out whatever plan God has for the universe while at the same time worshiping Him.

Along came Charles Darwin, who in 1859 published *On the Origin of Species*. He and his colleague Alfred Russel Wallace independently amassed a great deal of empirical evidence to buttress two revolutionary insights: first, that all species on earth are related by common descent, like people in a family tree, with brothers and sisters, cousins, uncles, and grandparents, reaching all the way back to the origin of life; and second, that the bewildering variety of living forms on earth, so exquisitely adapted to their diverse living conditions, are the result of a fundamental process that they called "natural selection." This process—which has been studied and documented in both the field and the laboratory ever since—works according to a remarkably simple algorithm. To begin with, Darwin and Wallace noted that natural populations of animals and plants always harbor a degree of variation in the characteristics of the individuals that make up those populations: some are shorter, some taller; some produce greener leaves, others less so; some are characterized by a fast metabolism, others by a slower one; and so on. Second, it is often the case that distinct variants of any given trait are more or less favorable in the particular environment in which the organism happens to live. So, for instance, leaves of a certain shape are more suited to life in the desert, where there is plenty of light but little water, while differently shaped leaves are better adapted to life on the floor of the rain forest, where water is abundant but light is scarce. In other words, these characteristics affect the two things that really matter—biologically speaking—for any living being on the planet: its survival and, even more crucially, its ability to reproduce. Finally, there is a correlation between the characteristics of parents and their offspring, because some traits are passed from generation to generation. (Darwin didn't know how this occurred, though the basic principle had been discovered at about the same time by Gregor Mendel, whose work was not appreciated until 1900.)

If we combine these three elements—variation plus differential fitness plus inheritance—we can deduce that, on average, fitter individuals are more likely to survive and to produce more offspring, thus spreading their characteristics throughout the population, at least until the environment changes and begins to favor different characteristics. At that point, the process—which we call "evolution by natural selection"—takes a new direction and continues on.

What does any of this have to do with human nature? The Darwinian theory of evolution struck a deathblow to any account of humanity based on *essential* characteristics, like the ones that both Aristotle and the Stoics (and pretty much everyone else in antiquity) put forth. Epictetus was certainly right when he told me: "From what does the rational element distinguish us? From wild beasts. And from what else? From sheep and the like." People are very different from "wild beasts" and sheep. But are we so different from other primates, particularly the great apes? Not really, according to modern biology. Our genome, to take one measure of things, differs from that of chimpanzees by 4 to 5 percent. That is still a lot, evolutionarily speaking, but I'm betting Aristotle would have been surprised by how small that percentage is. Moreover, biologists have systematically been finding that a long list of allegedly unique human traits are actually not unique to us at all. We are not the only animals to live in cooperatively social groups, nor the only ones to use tools. Nor are we the only species with complex communication abilities, nor even the only ones displaying what we would call moral behavior (which can be seen among bonobos and other primates).

That said, we do seem to be the only animals who use language featuring complex grammar, have babies who are born with very large brains and continue to grow them long after birth, and have highly asymmetrical brain hemispheres, which are specialized for different functions (including, very importantly, language in the left one). We also have the largest brain-to-body ratio in the mammalian world, and—this is an odd one—we are the only ape or Old World monkey without a bone in our penis.

Looking at this (incomplete) list, you will notice that most of the entries are quantitative, not qualitative. Our brains are *larger* and *more* asymmetrical, our babies are *bigger* and grow *longer* after birth, and so forth. That is, these are differences of degree, not kind, between us and other animals. Other entries seem to be irrelevant to the point that Aristotle and the Stoics were making: okay, we don't have a penis bone, but that hardly has anything to do with our rational faculties, philosophizing, or virtue. Perhaps our most promising distinguishing trait is language, though even there people disagree on what exactly constitutes a language, as distinct from other means of signaling and communication.

But my rejection of biology-based skepticism about human nature does not hinge on the quixotic search for a human essence. On the contrary, it is based on embracing the findings of modern biology and taking them seriously. Research has indeed shown that most or all characteristics separating different species of living beings, including our own, are quantitative, lying along a multidimensional continuum. But it has also clearly demonstrated that individual members of the same species of complex, multicellular organisms—and particularly vertebrates, of which we are an example—cluster much more tightly together on that multidimensional continuum than they come close to similar clusters of different species (with exceptions, because as every biologist will readily tell you, the only law in biology is that one can always find exceptions). This is a fancy way to say that you look and behave like a member of the species *Homo sapiens,* and that it doesn't take a biologist to tell you apart from your closest evolutionary kin, *Pan troglodytes* (the chimpanzee). That is really all we need to know to meaningfully talk about human nature: human beings are sufficiently different from closely related species as to have their own multidimensional set of distinguishing characteristics, and it just so happens that a number of these traits have to do with our incredibly enhanced ability for social cooperation, as well as with our gigantic brain power. And it is precisely these two aspects of humanity—sociability and reason—that the Stoics insisted on as the basis for their claim of human exceptionalism.

So much for the biology of human nature. But recently the idea of humans' exceptionalness hasn't fared well in some quarters of the humanities either, especially in philosophy. The objections come from two lines of reasoning, which we need to briefly examine before we can go back to our friend

Epictetus. Some philosophers simply deploy the same argument we have just examined, arguing that Darwin dealt a deathblow to the idea of essentialism. Other philosophers take the opposite route, relying not on genetics but on cultural anthropology to conclude that humanity is so flexible in its behavior and encompasses so much variability even across human cultures in both space and time that we simply cannot meaningfully talk about a unified concept of human nature.

The latter argument is a bit strange on two counts. First, if in fact human culture was *that* variable, then that in itself would be a unique characteristic in the animal world and would help—somewhat paradoxically—to distinguish humans from other species. Second, and a bit more seriously, all human beings do share quite a few traits that do not appear to be variable across cultures—an indication that human behavioral plasticity is indeed limited. Some of these shared traits include using a calendar (that is, purposefully keeping track of time), developing a cosmology (explaining how the world is and how it came about), engaging in divination, conducting funeral rites, adopting rules for the inheritance of property, joking, displaying customs related to puberty, having a concept of a soul or something like one, and tool-making. (Note that this list is distinct from the list of characteristics that *only* humans have; for instance, other species also engage in tool-making, of a sort.)

In the end, it seems that neither biological variation nor cultural diversity can be reasonably deployed to reject what the ancients thought was obvious: we are a very different species from anything else that planet Earth has produced over billions of years of evolution, both for better (our stunning cultural and technological achievements) and for worse (the environmental destruction and the pain and suffering we have imposed on other species as well as on our own). In particular—and this is the crucial point of interest to us here—what makes us so different is not something as trivial as the absence of a bone. Rather, it is our social and mental abilities—the very abilities that make it possible for me to write the book you are reading, and that make you care about reading it.

We are now in a much better position to more accurately parse Epictetus's response to the questions with which we began this chapter: "For what is Man? A rational animal, subject to death. At once we ask, from what does the rational element distinguish us? From wild beasts. And from what else? From sheep and the like." His explanation to me continued: "See that you do not act like a sheep, or else again the Man in you perishes. You ask how we act like sheep? When we consult the belly, or our passions, when our actions are random or dirty or inconsiderate, are we not falling away to the state of sheep? What do we destroy? The faculty of reason. When our actions are combative, mischievous, angry, and rude, do we not fall away and become wild beasts?" Epictetus is affirming that what distinguishes humankind from all other species is our capacity for rationality and arguing for an ethical precept as a result: we *ought* not to behave like beasts or sheep because doing so negates our very humanity, presumably the most precious (and natural!) thing we have. Perhaps you can begin to see why "following nature" has nothing to do with tree-hugging.

But now we have another problem, philosophically speaking. Are Epictetus and his fellow Stoics committing an elementary logical fallacy known as making an "appeal to nature"? In other words, are they arguing that something is good *because* it is natural, never mind that a good number of natural things are actually quite bad for us? (Poisonous mushrooms come to mind.) The problematic appeal to nature in the specific case of ethics has a long history, which was crystallized by one of the major figures of the Enlightenment, the Scottish philosopher David Hume. He observed what he thought was a peculiar behavior:

> In every system of morality, which I have hitherto met with, I have always remarked, that the author proceeds for some time in the ordinary ways of reasoning, and establishes the being of a God, or makes observations concerning human affairs; when all of a sudden I am surprised to find, that instead of the usual copulations of propositions, is, and is not, I meet with no proposition that is not connected with an ought, or an ought not. This change is imperceptible; but is however, of the last consequence. For as this ought, or ought not, expresses some new relation or affirmation, 'tis necessary that it should be observed and explained; and at the same time that a reason should be given, for what seems altogether inconceivable, how this new relation can be a deduction from others, which are entirely different from it.

This is now a classic passage in philosophy, and the problem Hume is referring to is aptly called the is/ought gap. He is interpreted by some people (those who emphasize "what seems altogether inconceivable, how this new relation can be a deduction from others") as saying that the gap *cannot* be bridged, while others more modestly claim that he simply said that *if* an attempt is made to bridge the gap, such a move needs to be justified (as in "'tis necessary that it should be observed and explained; and at the same time that a reason should be given"). Regardless of what Hume actually meant, I lean toward the second position. It seems to me that ethics has to come from somewhere, and a naturalistic account of it is the most promising approach. It is also the approach used by all the Greco-Roman philosophies, and by Stoicism in particular.

In modern discussions of the roots of morality, there are, roughly speaking, four ways to look at the issue, or what philosophers refer to as "meta-ethical" positions: one can be a skeptic, a rationalist, an empiricist, or an intuitionist. If you are a skeptic in this context, you are basically saying that there is no way to know which ethical judgments are right or not. Often moral skeptics claim that when people say, for instance, that "murder is wrong," they are committing a special kind of error (known as a category mistake): mixing up things that don't belong to each other, like a statement of fact (a murder was committed) and a value judgment (something is wrong). Clearly, skeptics think that the is/ought gap cannot be bridged, and that indeed facts have nothing whatsoever to do with judgments. Needless to say, moral skeptics are not popular at dinner parties.

Rationalism is a general position in philosophy that maintains that it is possible to arrive at knowledge by just thinking about stuff, as opposed to observing or experimenting. Although this plays into the stereotype of the so-called armchair philosopher, don't laugh too quickly: logicians and mathematicians produce new knowledge by rationalist means all the time, so the question really is whether ethics is anything like mathematics or logic. Some people think so, while others disagree.

Often counterposed against rationalism is empiricism, the stance that we ultimately arrive at knowledge on the basis of empirical facts—that is, observations and experiments. Science is the ultimate empiricist discipline of course, so to say that ethical knowledge can be arrived at empirically is to attempt to somehow bridge the is/ought gap in a scientifically based way.

Finally, we have intuitionism, the proposition that ethical knowledge does not require any kind of inference, whether by way of reason or observation. Instead, it is sort of built into us in the form of strong intuitions about what is right and wrong. How might that be? Well, for instance, I mentioned that other primates exhibit proto-moral behaviors, such as helping nonkin who appear to be in danger or distress. Presumably bonobo chimpanzees don't exhibit this behavior because they have read philosophical treatises on right and wrong. They simply act instinctively, and that instinct was probably built into them by natural selection because it fosters prosocial behavior, which is crucial for the survival of small groups of primates. Because we share a recent common ancestor with the bonobos, and because our own ancestors also lived in small bands in which prosocial behavior was adaptive, it is not too much of a stretch to think that we do indeed have a moral instinct, and that we have inherited it from primates that preceded us.

The Stoic approach to ethics is interesting because it doesn't actually fit these four neat categories. Indeed, Stoic doctrine can be thought of as a combination of intuitionism, empiricism, and rationalism. The Stoics, however, were most definitely not skeptics. Stoics held a "developmental" theory of ethical concern, according to which we begin life guided only by instincts (not reason), and those instincts favor both self-regard and regard for the people with whom we interact daily, usually our parents, siblings, and more or less extended family. Up to that point, we are essentially behaving like pure intuitionists, with our ethical intuitions built into our very nature as humans.

Gradually, we are taught to expand our concern as we approach the age of reason—roughly speaking, when we are six-to eight-year-old children. At that point, we begin to make clearer distinctions between our thoughts and our actions and to have a better grasp of the world and of our place in it. From this point on, our instincts are enhanced, and sometimes even corrected, by a combination of self-reflection and experience—that is, by both rationalist and empiricist processes. The Stoics thought that the more we mature psychologically and intellectually the more the balance *should* shift away from our instincts and toward the deployment of (empirically informed) reasoning. During our conversation, Epictetus explained to me that it is "the nature of the rational animal, that he can attain nothing good for himself, unless he contributes some service to the community. So it turns out that to do everything for his own sake is not unsocial." That brought us back to human nature: Epictetus was telling me that a fundamental aspect of being human is that we are social, not just in the sense that we *like* the company of others, but in the deeper sense that we couldn't really exist without the help of others; the implication is that when we do things for the good of the polity, we are actually (perhaps indirectly) benefiting ourselves. This is a remarkably insightful account of humanity, one that fits well with the discovery, sixteen centuries after Epictetus, that human beings in fact evolved as a type of social primate, sharing adaptive prosocial instincts with our cousins on the evolutionary tree.

But it is another second-century Stoic philosopher, Hierocles, who perhaps best synthesized the school's thinking on these matters in his *Elements of Ethics,* of which, unfortunately, only fragments remain. (We also don't know much about Hierocles himself, except that Aulus Gellius described him as a "grave and holy man.") Here is how he puts it:

> Each of us is, as it were, circumscribed by many circles. . . . The first, indeed, and most proximate circle is that which everyone describes about his own mind as a centre. . . . The second from this, and which is at a greater distance from the centre, but comprehends the first circle, is that in which parents, brothers, wife, and children are arranged. . . . Next to this is that which contains the common people, then that which comprehends those of the same tribe, afterwards that which contains the citizens. . . . But the outermost and greatest circle, and which comprehends all the other circles, is that of the whole human race. . . . It is the province of him who strives to conduct himself properly in each of these connections to collect, in a certain respect, the circles, as it were, to one

centre, and always to endeavor earnestly to transfer himself from the comprehending circles to the several particulars which they comprehend.

Being a Stoic, and hence of a practical bent, Hierocles even suggested how to behave in a way that helps us internalize the concept that the people in the various circles are of concern to us. For instance, he advised his students to refer to strangers as "brother" or "sister" or, if they were older, as "uncle" or "aunt," as a constant reminder that we should treat other people as if they really are our relatives, as reason counsels that we are all in the same boat together, so to speak.

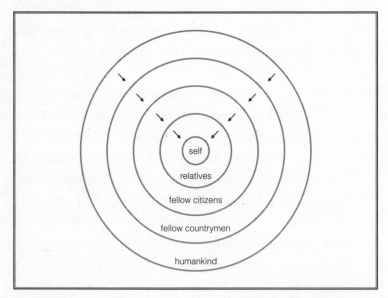

FIGURE 4.1. The Stoic idea of cosmopolitanism, visualized as contracting circles of concern, according to the second-century philosopher Hierocles. The idea is to train ourselves to treat people in the outer circles the way we treat people from the inner circles.

Even today a number of cultures have similar customs, having independently arrived at Hierocles's insight into human psychology.

The Stoics perfected this idea of ethical development and called it *oikeiôsis*, which is often translated as "familiarization with" or "appropriation of" other people's concerns as if they were our own. This led them (and the Cynics who immediately preceded them and influenced them greatly) to coin and use a word that is still crucial to our modern vocabulary: cosmopolitanism, which literally means "being a citizen of the world." Or as Socrates—arguably the most important influence on all Hellenistic schools of philosophy—put it: "Never . . . reply to one who asks [your] country, 'I am an Athenian,' or 'I am a Corinthian,' but 'I am a citizen of the universe.'"

CHAPTER 5

PLAYING BALL WITH SOCRATES

Material things are indifferent, but how we handle them is
not indifferent.

—EPICTETUS, *DISCOURSES*, II.5

WHEN WE TALKED ABOUT "LIVING ACCORDING TO NATURE"
in the previous chapter, I mentioned that the Stoics had a
fondness for pithy summaries of their philosophy. I find this
to be an endearing aspect of their thinking, for a couple of
reasons. First, it is a forceful reminder that they were interested in practice, not just theory: their aphorisms were meant
to benefit the *prokoptôn,* that is, to help the student of Stoicism make progress. Unlike modern bumper stickers, T-shirt
slogans, and so forth, which primarily signal membership
in a particular group and tend to be used as a metaphorical
club with which to beat those who are not like-minded, Stoic
stock phrases were employed by practitioners as personal reminders, as aids for daily meditation, or as a guide to behavior
when they were in doubt. Stoicism, in other words, was not
meant to be worn on your sleeve (unless you were someone,
say a teacher, who couldn't avoid doing so). Marcus Aurelius

carried this attitude to the extreme: his famous *Meditations* were written as a personal diary of reflection, not as a book meant for publication, and in antiquity the work was known as *Ta Eis Heauton,* which simply means "To Himself."

I also like Stoic aphorisms because these short sentences are often superficially paradoxical and can be taken in one of two ways: on the one hand, as a perennial source of frustration, since the Stoic must constantly explain herself to others who keep misunderstanding what her philosophy is about, and on the other hand, as an opportunity for a teaching moment: asked about one of these "paradoxes," the Stoic has the perfect opening to move from the bumper sticker level to at least the level of an elevator speech, which seems to be the most that much modern conversation allows, be it in person or on social media.

Perhaps the most paradoxical of these phrases is "preferred indifferents" (and "dispreferred indifferents"). Since the category "indifferent" pretty much encompasses *everything* outside of an individual's excellence of character, or virtue, then we better get clear on what exactly the Stoics meant by this.

As usual, I asked Epictetus to clarify, this time during a nice walk in the Casal Palocco area of Rome, where there happens to be a street named after him. (That surprised the hell out of my friend, who is very modest by nature.) As he often does, he referred me to Socrates, who was a major influence on Stoic thought: "[Socrates] was like one playing at ball. What then was the ball that he played with? Life, imprisonment, exile, taking poison, being deprived of his wife, leaving his children orphans. These were the things he played with, but none the less he played and tossed the ball with balance.

So we ought to play the game, so to speak, with all possible care and skill, but treat the ball itself as indifferent."

Let me unpack this analogy, which is clearly between one's life and playing ball. I'm not sure which game Epictetus was referring to, but let's say it was Greco-Roman soccer. The point of the analogy is that the ball itself, though central to the game and apparently the focus of everyone's attention, is actually indifferent—meaning that it could take a variety of colors and shapes, be made of different materials, or be of different sizes, but it isn't valuable in itself. The ball is only a means to an end and isn't the important thing—it is what one *does* with the ball that defines the game, how well it is played, and who wins or loses. Indeed, a good player does not have rigid ideas about how to handle the ball, when or to whom to pass it, and so on. The best players are those who display *fantasia* (creativity), who are imaginative about what they do on the field, and who find new ways to turn difficult situations to their favor, making the obstacle the way, to paraphrase Marcus Aurelius. Moreover, the hallmark of an admirable player isn't that he wins games, but that he plays his best regardless of the final outcome, which, after all, is not under his control.

Likewise with Socrates: Fate handed him certain materials to play with, including the time and place of his birth, the political system and situation of Athens in the fifth century BCE, and so forth. He strove to live a good life, doing his military duty during the Peloponnesian War and teaching his fellow citizens about philosophy. When Meletus, with the shady support of Anytus and Lycon, accused him of "impiety" (that is, not believing in the state's official gods), he stood in front of his fellow citizens to argue his case—even though it was clear that the charges stemmed from a combination of political and personal vendettas on the part of his accusers.

After he was condemned to death by the tribunal of the people, Socrates had an easy opportunity to escape thanks to his friends, who were more than willing to bribe the guards (a rather common practice, and not only in those times). Instead, he turned the occasion into an explanation of his duties toward the city that had given him birth and nurtured him his whole life. In Plato's *Crito*, Socrates tells his distraught friends that he has a moral duty to accept the law even when it is patently misused, because we don't get to change the rules when they happen not to suit us. He is therefore willing to take the poison and leave his friends, students, wife, and child in order not to compromise his integrity, which is the important thing; all else is "indifferent," not in the sense that Socrates didn't care about his friends and family (or, for that matter, his own life), but in the deeper sense that he was not willing to compromise his virtue in order to save his skin, or even to spare his loved ones suffering. As Epictetus told me during our conversation: "How do I know what is going to turn up? My business is to use what does turn up with diligence and skill. . . . It is for you, then, to take what is given you and make the most of it."

A modern-day analogy may be made here with the American whistleblower Edward Snowden. As is well known, Snowden was a contractor for the US National Security Agency. In 2013 he released a number of classified documents that exposed a broad, and arguably illegal, surveillance system enacted by the NSA, which has since led to a much-needed debate on the balance between surveillance and democratic values in an open society. Predictably, the very mention of Snowden tends to generate polarized responses, just as Socrates's name did in his time: for some he is a hero, for others a traitor, and in fact he may well be considered both. Quite irrespectively of whether what Snowden did was morally right or not—again, similar to the question of whether Socrates's teachings and political actions were right or not—we can reasonably wonder about the ethics of Snowden seeking asylum abroad (at the moment of this writing in Russia, of all places) rather than facing the two charges of violating the 1917 Espionage Act that the US government has leveled against him. I honestly do not know the answer. Socrates decided to stay, and Snowden decided not to return, but even if you think that Snowden should have faced the consequences (right or not) of his actions, we can all probably agree that few people have risen to the moral stature of Socrates—which is why he is one of the standard role models used by Stoics.

Luckily, most of us will not face the morally treacherous terrain on which Socrates and Snowden found themselves. Nonetheless, we have plenty of opportunities to decide how to play the balls thrown in our direction by life. Let me give you a couple of trivial examples. Not long after my conversation with Epictetus, I happened to need some cash for personal expenses, so I went around the corner from my apartment in New York, accessed the ATM of the local branch of my bank, and got the money. And then I froze in my tracks. You see, if you hang around Stoics, you soon discover that *everything* has an ethical dimension. In this case, I suddenly remembered that my bank had notoriously been involved in a number of shady practices (for example, questionable investments and financial tools), directed toward both their own employees and society at large. That meant that my preferred indifferent—being able to conveniently get cash from my account whenever I need it—was actually in tension with my implicit support of labor and social practices that I oppose in principle. Oops.

As a result of that reflection, I walked into the bank's branch and explained to a baffled customer representative that I was closing my account, not because I was dissatisfied with the level of service (which was actually excellent), but because I had irreconcilable differences with the bank about how they were using what was, after all, my money. I then did some research and found a bank that, though most certainly not ethically impeccable, was unquestionably better than the one I had just ditched. I brought my business to them, and I have been feeling a little better ever since.

Similarly, I grew up a complete omnivore in Italy, with parents and grandparents who couldn't really wrap their minds around the word "vegetarian." I am not a vegetarian even today, but I've gradually started paying more attention to where my food comes from, and at what cost in terms of animal suffering, environmental impact, and human labor. It is a complex problem, with no easy solution and plenty of conflicts among distinct indifferents. For instance, contra to the standard vegetarian argument, it is not at all easy to calculate just how many animals suffer and die when you take up a vegetarian diet, because large-scale cultivation of plant species for human consumption radically alters the environment of the planet, depriving a number of wild animal species of vital ecological space. If you think that eating local and organic is sustainable, you may be in for a surprise when you look at the relevant literature or do a bit of back-of-the-envelope calculation. Even the activist-journalist Michael Pollan, author of the best-selling *The Omnivore's Dilemma: A Natural History of Four Meals*, agrees that we cannot feed billions of people on the kind of diet that he and I can afford and easily find at our local green grocery shops. Then again, to argue that we have a right to eat whatever we fancy, regardless of the demonstrably immense levels of suffering and environmental damage we inflict in the process, seems more than a bit callous.

This dilemma is probably why a number of Stoics were in fact vegetarian. Take Seneca, who wrote that "I was imbued with this [vegetarian] teaching, and began to abstain from animal food; at the end of the year the habit was as pleasant as it was easy. I was beginning to feel that my mind was more active." Seneca eventually abandoned vegetarianism because he did not want to be associated with a particular political faction that had adopted the practice. Was he then just an opportunist, or at the very least morally weak? Not necessarily. We do not know the details, but he may have calculated that sticking to a vegetarian diet would have done less good for the world (which for him meant, of course, Roman society) than choosing to differentiate himself from that particular political party. Being vegetarian, in and of itself, is no proof of superior moral quality, but it is a good thing to do *if* other considerations do not outweigh that choice. And it is the hallmark of a wise person to be able to navigate a complex situation otherwise characterized by no easily identifiable, optimal course of action.

Musonius Rufus, Epictetus's teacher, was famous for being a particularly practical Stoic who gave his students advice on everything from the important things in life (such as the idea that women ought to get the same education as men) to somewhat trivial matters, like how to furnish your house (efficiently, with stuff that doesn't break easily) or cut your hair (removing only what is useless). He had a lot to say about diet too. He argued that "although there are many pleasures which persuade human beings to do wrong and compel them to act against their own interests, the pleasure connected with food is undoubtedly the most difficult of all pleasures to combat," adding: "To obtain those few moments of gastronomic pleasure, countless expensive foods must be prepared and brought overseas from distant lands. Cooks are more highly valued than farmers. Some people spend all their possessions to have their banquets prepared, but they are not made stronger by eating these expensive foods. . . . When it comes to food, responsible people favor what is easy to obtain over what is difficult, what involves no trouble over what does, and what is available over what isn't."

Now this strikes very close to home for me, and it is an excellent example of how the Stoics saw life's preferred indifferents. As I mentioned, I grew up in Rome and live in New York. Indeed, I am writing this book during a sabbatical from my home institution, a leave of absence that I'm spending in the Eternal City, partly to get inspired by almost daily walks to the Colosseum, the Forum, and other sights, but partly to enjoy the company of my family and, yes, the delicious food my hometown readily offers! My partner and I also take advantage of all the good restaurants in the Big Apple, including a number of expensive ones where the cooks are definitely better paid than the farmers and where, to obtain a few moments of gastronomic pleasure, countless expensive foods must be prepared and brought overseas from distant lands. It seems like my choices at this point are rather limited, and somewhat unpleasant: either I should frankly admit that for all this talk about Stoicism, I'm actually an epicurean (in the modern, small-*e* sense of the word) and therefore a hypocrite, or I should give up fine dining in the name of logical consistency, thus relegating myself to what others may consider a joyless life while surrounded by culinary pleasures of all kinds in which I refuse to partake.

But one of the first things you learn if you study philosophy is that there rarely is such a thing as a sharp dichotomy in any but the more trivial matters. In fact, when I teach informal logic, I warn my students that more often than not, if someone is presenting them with just one of two forced choices, that person is probably committing what is called the fallacy of false dichotomy—he's not telling them that other options are available. (Of course, in some cases there really are only two options, and being forced to face a narrow choice is no logical error, but the general point holds.) In this case, for instance, cheap, delicious, *and* healthy meals can be found in Rome, prepared by local cooks using seasonally available ingredients—thus satisfying Musonius's requirements. It is also possible to find such meals in New York, of course, but there the temptation to splurge on seriously (perhaps outrageously) expensive meals, which are far better described as "culinary experiences," is great. That is where I decided to draw the line, within limits. I told my partner and my closest friends that I'd rather not go to, say, Eleven Madison Park, if it could be avoided. Which of course is possible most of the time. But not all the time: if a dear friend, or my companion, were to tell me that once in a lifetime they really want to have the Eleven Madison Park experience—say, to celebrate a very special occasion—and would be greatly disappointed if I didn't join them, I might consider it. That's not hypocrisy or rationalization, I think, but rather a balancing of competing demands that stem from different ethical criteria: supporting a type of operation of which I do not approve versus disappointing someone I love. (Remember that I am using the Greco-Roman understanding of "ethics," which had a much broader meaning than the modern word.) The reasonable thing to do—and Stoics were all about applying reason to everyday affairs—might be to compromise: yes, we'll go this one time, but we'll make up for it in some fashion, like doubling our efforts to patronize locally sourced and environmentally and labor friendly eateries for the rest of the year. Will I feel uncomfortable during that evening of celebration? Probably, but as the emperor Marcus Aurelius said—and he wasn't kidding or being sarcastic—"If [you] must live in a palace, then [you] can also live well in a palace."

Generally speaking, then, Stoic ethics isn't just about what we do—our actions—but more broadly about how our character is equipped to navigate real life. We live in far too intricate social environments to be able to always do the right thing, or even to do the right thing often enough to *know* with sufficient confidence what the right thing is to begin with. Most of the different demands made on us have an ethical dimension (animal suffering, environmental damage, the treatment of waiters), but some are also more practical (I need to eat, but where is my food coming from? I need to bank, but which bank am I supporting?). Stoicism is about developing the tools to deal as effectively as humanly possible with the ensuing conflicts, does not demand perfection, and does not provide specific answers: those are for fools (Epictetus's word) who think the world is black and white, good versus evil, where it is always possible to clearly tell the good guys from the bad guys. That is not the world we live in, and to pretend otherwise is more than a bit dangerous and not at all wise.

That said, let me return to the idea of indifferents, and their classification as "preferred" or "dispreferred," by contrasting Stoicism with two other important Hellenistic schools of thought: Aristotelianism and Cynicism (the latter being a word that, even more so than Stoicism and Epicureanism, has a different meaning today than it did then—which is why I capitalize the words in reference to the philosophies and lowercase them otherwise).

Aristotle was a student of Plato (and hence a grandstudent of Socrates, so to speak), and his philosophy was characterized by a very practical, if somewhat elitist, approach. In his version of virtue ethics, a eudaimonic life is made possible by the pursuit of virtue, but we also need many other things over which we have no control: health, wealth, education, and even good looks.

Contrast this with the thinking of the first Cynic, Antisthenes, himself a student of Socrates. Antisthenes, and even more so his famous successor, Diogenes of Sinope, went radical: for them, *nothing* is necessary for a eudaimonic life except virtue. We may be healthy or sick, wealthy or poor, educated or ignorant, handsome or ugly—none of it matters. Indeed, they went so far as to argue that earthly possessions positively get in the way of virtue: they develop in us an attachment to things that don't matter, so we are better off without them.

Diogenes seriously practiced what he preached. His lifestyle could be characterized as in-your-face ascetic, as he made a show of sleeping in a tub in the streets of Athens, defecating and copulating in public (hence the term "Cynic," which means doglike), and carrying little or nothing for his own survival and comfort. There are wonderful stories about Diogenes. One tells us that he was thirsty one day, and so pulled out a bowl while approaching some running water. He then saw a boy helping himself to the water by simply cupping his hands to hold the liquid. Diogenes threw away his bowl in disgust, muttering that even a boy was wiser than him. On another occasion, he was visited by Alexander the Great, who had heard of the famous philosopher and went to pay his respects (presumably, in front of the tub). When Alexander magnanimously (or so he thought) asked Diogenes what he, the most powerful man in the world, could do on behalf of the philosopher, the latter looked up and said something along the lines of "you could move, you are blocking my sun." That ought to give you an idea of why the Cynics were both much admired and much despised.

Now here is the problem: On the one hand, we have Aristotle telling us that eudaimonia can be achieved only by somewhat lucky people who fit a number of prerequisites, acquired through little or no merit of their own. On the other hand, we've got the Cynics not only rejecting Aristotle's list of necessary prerequisites but arguing that they *get in the way* of a good life. Stoics occupy the logical space in between these two positions: health, wealth, education, and good looks—among

other things—are preferred indifferents, while their oppo-
sites—and a number of other things—are dispreferred indifferents. This, I think, was a stroke of genius. The Stoics made
a eudaimonic life a reachable goal for everyone, regardless of
social status, financial resources, physical health, or degree of
attractiveness. Although all of these qualities are indifferent
to your ability to pursue a virtuous life—to become a morally
worthy person—they are still preferred (just as any normal
human being would readily tell you) so long as they don't get
in the way of your practice of the virtues. Here is how Seneca
aptly summarized the idea in the case of a particularly common contrast between preferred and dispreferred experiences:
"There is great difference between joy and pain; if I am asked
to choose, I shall seek the former and avoid the latter. The former is according to nature, the latter contrary to it. So long as
they are rated by this standard, there is a great gulf between;
but when it comes to a question of the virtue involved, the
virtue in each case is the same, whether it comes through joy
or through sorrow." In other words, by all means go ahead
and avoid pain and experience joy in your life—but not when
doing so imperils your integrity. Better to endure pain in an
honorable manner than to seek joy in a shameful one.

There is a way to understand this point in very modern parlance, using the language of economic theory, of all
things. Economists have developed the concept of lexicographic preferences, so called because they work in a fashion
similar to the ordering of words in a dictionary to describe
situations where people want incommensurable goods—that
is, goods that cannot be compared to each other in terms of
value. Let's say that I value goods 1 and 2, which belong to

category A, but also goods 3, 4, and 5, which belong to category B. While 1 and 2 can be compared and contrasted, and the same goes for 3, 4, and 5, no good belonging to A is comparable to any good belonging to B, and anything from A has complete precedence over anything from B. The result is that goods can be traded *within* either A or B, but not across these categories. Here the pursuit of virtue is in category A, while the preferred indifferents are in category B. Within B, you may well trade things off: money for education, a good career for family life, and so forth. But for a Stoic, there is no trade-off between A and B: *nothing* can be traded if the price is the compromising of your character. This, incidentally, means that there are contrasts between goods—such as virtue versus physical health—to which standard economic theory simply does not apply.

This may sound strange, but a moment's reflection will show that we all already use lexicographic indexing for many of our choices. You might like, say, the idea of going on vacation in a nice resort in the Caribbean. And because going on vacation and spending money are on the same lexicographical level, you are willing to trade off some of your hard-earned money in order to achieve that goal. But I assume that you wouldn't sell your daughter for any purpose at all, and certainly not just to enjoy a vacation. That's because your daughter belongs to a higher lexicographical level, one that is incommensurable with vacations, as pleasant and needed as the latter may be.

Regardless of whether we express it in philosophical or economic terms, this Stoic concept is quite empowering. If you follow Aristotle (and, let's be frank, a lot of what passes for common sense), you need to be part of the lucky elite or you won't have a good life. This outlook puts most people on the perennially losing side of things, condemning them to the pursuit of material goods because they mistakenly think that their happiness and worth depend on acquiring them. Psychologists call this the hedonic treadmill: you keep running, but you ain't goin' nowhere. By contrast, everyone can have a good life according to the Cynics, but few of us are inclined to spend it living in a tub and defecating in the streets. The Stoic compromise—their lexicographic contrast between the virtues and the preferred indifferents, coupled with their treatment of the two as hierarchically ordered, incommensurable classes of goods—brilliantly overcomes the problem, retaining the best of both (philosophical) worlds.

CHAPTER 6

GOD OR ATOMS?

What then is the nature of God? Is it flesh? God forbid.
Land? God forbid. Fame? God forbid.
It is intelligence, knowledge, right reason.
In these then and nowhere else seek the true nature of the
good.

—EPICTETUS, *DISCOURSES*, II.8

I DO HAVE A MAJOR DISAGREEMENT WITH MY FRIEND EPICtetus, and yet the fact that we can have such diverging opinions on a fundamental matter and still see eye to eye about how to live our lives is one of the most precious features of Stoicism: it makes room for both religious believers and unbelievers, united by their common understanding of ethics regardless of their diverging metaphysics.

When I asked Epictetus about his view of God, he replied: "Who is it that has fitted the sword to the scabbard and the scabbard to the sword? Is there no one? Surely the very structure of such finished products leads us commonly to infer that they must be the work of some craftsman, and are not constructed at random. Are we to say then that each of these products points to the craftsman, but that things visible and vision and light do not? Do not male and female and the desire of union and the power to use the organs adapted for it—do not these point to the craftsman?" This is a remarkable early example (since it was written in the second century CE) of what is known as the argument from design to support the existence of God. A variation of it was later used by prominent Christian theologians, such as Thomas Aquinas, and it is perhaps best known in the formulation of the nineteenth-century natural theologian William Paley, who articulated it just a few decades before Darwin wrote *On the Origin of Species:*

> In crossing a heath, suppose I pitched my foot against a stone, and were asked how the stone came to be there; I might possibly answer, that, for anything I knew to the contrary, it had lain there forever: nor would it perhaps be very easy to show the absurdity of this answer. But suppose I had found a watch upon the ground, and it should be inquired how the watch happened to be in that place; I should hardly think of the answer I had before given, that for anything I knew, the watch might have always been there. . . . There must have existed, at some time, and at some place or other, an artificer or artificers, who formed [the watch] for the purpose which we find it actually to answer; who comprehended its construction, and designed its use. . . . Every indication of contrivance, every manifestation of design, which existed in the watch, exists in the works of nature; with the difference, on the side of nature, of being greater or more, and that in a degree which exceeds all computation.

The argument is intuitively very powerful, and likely to be brought up by most believers as a first response to the question of why they believe. It is also, predictably, the argument against which atheists have often concentrated most of their firepower. It is not my intention to convince the reader one way or the other, as this book isn't about apologetics, and even less so about atheism. I would be intellectually dishonest, however, if I did not put forth my own opinion, just as I did during my friendly chat with Epictetus. This is what good philosophers—and reasonable people in general—are supposed to do: listen to each other's arguments, learn and reflect, and go out for a beer to talk it over some more.

My considered opinion is that Epictetus's argument (and Aquinas's and Paley's) was eminently reasonable until sometime between the eighteenth and nineteenth centuries. What happened then was that two brilliant minds, one a philosopher, the other a scientist, dealt a powerful double punch to the argument from design. Those punches did not deliver a win by knockout (that rarely happens in philosophy), but I think the argument, though still vigorously defended by a number of theologians, philosophers, and even some scientists, has lost a significant amount of its appeal.

The first cogent attack on the argument from design came from David Hume, who wrote: "If we see a house . . . we conclude, with the greatest certainty, that it had an architect or builder because this is precisely that species of effect which we have experienced to proceed from that species of cause. But surely you will not affirm that the universe bears such a resemblance to a house that we can with the same certainty infer a similar cause, or that the analogy is here entire and perfect."

Hume's point is subtle but crucial: he is basically saying that arguments from analogies, of which the one from design is an example, are notoriously problematic because analogies are always imperfect, and in some cases downright misleading.

More precisely, Hume acknowledges that if we see a manufactured object, we are justified in inferring the existence of a human maker, but only because we have actually seen, or have otherwise incontrovertible evidence of, people making things. In the case of the universe, however, we have never seen one being created, nor do we have any knowledge of the existence of a Creator to begin with—indeed, that is precisely the point under contention: how did the cosmos come about? Moreover, if a Creator does exist, we have no idea of its attributes. Accordingly, Hume continued with a bit of mischievousness (which was dangerous at the time when he was writing). If we take the analogy between human and cosmic designers seriously, he argued, then we have to conclude that the latter have the following properties: there are many of them, they are fallible, and they are mortal—all suggestions that do not go at all well with a standard Christian theological account of God.

Although Hume developed a powerful counterargument against the appeal to design—one that is still studied in introductory philosophy courses today—he was missing something rather big: an alternative explanation for the undeniable *appearance* of design in the world, particularly the biological world. That missing piece was provided less than a century later by the great biologist Charles Darwin. His theory of evolution by natural selection is even now accepted as the scientific explanation of why eyes and hands and hearts and lungs do look like watches and swords, and yet are the product of natural phenomena that do not in fact require intelligent design. Moreover, Darwin combined his explanation of the appearance of design with the unanswered question of the existence of suffering in the world, another much-debated topic. As he explained in a famous letter: "But I own that I cannot see, as plainly as others do, & as I shd [sic] wish to do, evidence of design & beneficence on all sides of us. There seems to me too much misery in the world. I cannot persuade myself that a beneficent & omnipotent God would have designedly created the Ichneumonidae with the express intention of their feeding within the living bodies of caterpillars, or that a cat should play with mice. Not believing this, I see no necessity in the belief that the eye was expressly designed."

Of course, Epictetus had not read Hume or Darwin, so I pointed out especially the last passage to him, and he responded in quintessential Stoic fashion. Remembering that one day one of his students who had a wounded leg had complained about his injury—saying, "Am I then to have a maimed leg?"—he told me that his response had been, shall we say, rather matter-of-fact: "Slave, do you mean to arraign the universe for one wretched leg?" (Epictetus also often called me "slave," or "boy," which, though somewhat politically incorrect, I find both endearing and fundamentally unobjectionable: he himself was a slave, and I am indeed significantly younger than him!)

Since this is an important aspect of Stoic metaphysics, it is worth examining a bit more carefully. Although Epictetus was arguably the most religious Stoic on record, he certainly didn't think that God should concern Himself with every minutia pertaining to human affairs (much less with Ichneumonid insects, had he known about them), as is clear from his quip about the audaciousness of someone pretending that the whole universe should be rearranged so that his leg will not hurt. More importantly, many of the Stoics did not believe in anything like the modern monotheistic conception of God. Their preferred word for it was Logos, which can be interpreted as the Word of God (as the Christians who inherited a lot of Stoic philosophy did), or as a kind of Providence embedded in the very fabric of the universe, or even more simply as the rather straightforward observation that the cosmos can be understood rationally, regardless of how it came to be. Epictetus himself very clearly told his students that he did not think God was something external, something "out there": "You are a principal work, a fragment of God Himself, you have in yourself a part of Him. . . . You bear God about with you, poor wretch, and know it not. Do you think I speak of some external god of silver or gold?" In this sense, the Stoics can be thought of as pantheistic (or perhaps panentheistic)—that is, as believing that God *is* the universe itself and therefore we all partake in the divine nature. The only difference between human beings and other animals is that we are capable of the highest attribute of God/Universe: reason. That is why the proper way to live our lives is by using reason to tackle our problems.

This identification of God with Nature has a long history, and it was developed particularly by the influential seventeenth-century Dutch philosopher Baruch Spinoza. It is sometimes referred to as "Einstein's God," because a similar sentiment was expressed by the famous physicist. There are two related points to be noted about this conception of God: first, the divinity doesn't engage in miracles; this God does not suspend the laws of nature in order to intervene here and there to right local wrongs. Second, and relatedly, there is very little practical difference between this God and a simple acknowledgment (made by the Stoics) that the universe works through a web of cause and effect; this very modern concept is entirely compatible with the scientific view of the world as we understand it. Thus, we can similarly interpret Epictetus's somewhat flippant answer to the student with the maimed leg in two ways: either to mean that God concerns Himself with the workings of the universe as a whole, not of every specific part, and that it is therefore presumptuous to complain about one's own issues; or to mean that the wound resulted from a series of causes and effects that certainly did not have the student's well-being in mind when they occurred, so it is futile to remonstrate against the outcome. Either way, to ask for things to be otherwise would indeed be to pretend to arraign the universe for the sake of one wretched leg. Moreover, such a petition would of course be a flagrant violation of the principle of the dichotomy of control, which we have seen is fundamental to Epictetus's teachings.

Epictetus replied to me that he was aware of the different opinions concerning the gods, but insisted that he could make sense of only one of them:

> Concerning the gods there are some who say that the Divine does not exist, others that it exists but is inactive and indifferent and takes no thought for anything, others again that God does exist and take thought but only for

great things and things in the heavens, but for nothing on earth; and a fourth class say that God takes thought also for earthly and human things, but only in a general way, and has no care for individuals: and there is a fifth class, to whom belong Odysseus and Socrates, who say: "where'er I move / Thou seest me." For if there are no gods, how can following the gods be the end of man? If again there are gods, but they care for nothing, in that case too what good will it be to follow them?

As much as I admire the prose, here I reminded him that Stoicism does not actually maintain that the end of man is to follow the gods. That was *his* own version. What the Stoics, including Epictetus, said, as we have seen, is that we should live our lives while following *nature,* and it is reasonable to equate this with following the gods only once we have clarified the relationship between nature and the gods—which Epictetus never really did. In fact, there was disagreement on this point both among Stoics and between them and rival schools, such as the Epicureans. The followers of Epicurus are often portrayed as "atheists," but they were nothing of the kind. They were what we today would call deists, falling into the third group enumerated by Epictetus: according to them, God does exist, but He is immersed in the contemplation of divine things, paying no heed at all to earthly matters and human affairs. The world, for the Epicureans, is made of a chaos of atoms randomly bumping into each other, and while human beings are capable of using reason, their decisions and actions are still held hostage, not to a divine providence, but to the effects of physical forces.

Some Stoics conceded this possibility, and others went so far as to appropriate some of Epicurus's thoughts and maintain—correctly—that philosophy isn't religion, it has no sacred texts, and it does not follow unquestionable doctrines. On the contrary, as Seneca aptly put it, "That which is true is mine," meaning that a reasonable person makes truth her own, regardless of whether it comes from friends or foes.

One of the Stoics who agreed with Epictetus's general take on the divine, but was more open-minded than him on such matters, was none other than the emperor-philosopher Marcus Aurelius. It seems clear that Marcus believed in gods. On the one hand, it is possible to rationalize some of his generic references to them as not necessarily reflecting faith but rather a broad form of piety, as, for instance, when he wrote: "To the gods I am indebted for having good grandfathers, good parents, a good sister, good teachers, good associates, good kinsmen and friends, nearly everything good." On the other hand, however, he was pretty explicit in other places: "Since it is possible that you might depart from life this very moment, regulate every act and thought accordingly. But to go away from among men, if there are gods, is not a thing to be afraid of, for the gods will not involve you in evil; but if indeed they do not exist, or if they have no concern about human affairs, why would I wish to live in a universe devoid of gods or devoid of Providence? But in truth they do exist, and they do care for human things, and they have put all the means in man's power to enable him not to fall into real evils."

Then again, Marcus very explicitly says a surprisingly high number of times in the *Meditations* that it doesn't matter whether the universe is governed by a providential divinity (in whatever form) or by random chaos (as the Epicureans thought), thus showing himself to be less certain in questions of metaphysics than Epictetus. Here is a taste of what I mean: "You have embarked, made the voyage, and come to shore; get out. If indeed to another life, there is no want of gods, not even there. But if to a state without sensation, you will cease to be held by pains and pleasures." Or consider this: "Either there is a fatal necessity and invincible order, or a kind Providence, or a confusion without a purpose and without a director. If then there is an invincible necessity, why do you resist? But if there is a Providence that allows itself to be propitiated, make yourself worthy of the help of the divinity. But if there is a confusion without a governor, be content that in such a tempest you have yourself a certain ruling intelligence." It hardly gets more ecumenical than this!

Considering our discussion so far, you may have been wondering why—given Epictetus's insistent talk about God, contrasting so sharply with my own skepticism—I have chosen him as a companion for this voyage of exploration of Stoicism. Indeed, you might reasonably ask why someone who is nonreligious is interested in Stoicism at all, given what can charitably be described as the ambiguity of Stoics toward the divine. The answer goes to the heart of what I think makes Stoicism such an attractive philosophy for the twenty-first century.

I used to be a brash atheist, even before New Atheism was a thing. When I was living in Tennessee, secure in my conviction that creationists were little more than country bumpkins waiting to be enlightened by the worldly professor from Rome, I debated scores of people who believed the earth to be only a few thousand years old. But I was seriously mistaken.

Not about the age of the earth—on that count, I'm pretty confident of my science trumping their religious doctrine—but rather on the point of the whole exercise. The first time this struck me was after a debate with Duane Gish, then the vice president of the Institute for Creation Research (which, to be clear, does no such thing). I remember feeling quite smug after having scored, or so I thought, a couple of really good rhetorical blows against Gish that evening. But after the debate I was approached by a number of people from his side who behaved very politely toward me and said: "You know, I still don't believe you are right and the Bible wrong, but I appreciated tonight that you were nice and correct while debating Dr. Gish." I hadn't made an impression on these folks by way of my astute science-based arguments, but simply by showing up and behaving like a decent human being rather than the prick they expected.

That point has been reiterated for me countless times now over the course of several encounters with a number of believers, both Christians and those of other persuasions. Moreover, I have learned that most of the time there is precious little difference between my actual conduct and their own in the business of everyday life. And if we are talking about mainstream religionists, as opposed to fundamentalists, our opinions on most crucial matters of ethics and politics are rarely that different—despite the fact that mine are allegedly informed by my atheism and theirs by their faith. To put it in philosophical terms, it appears that much of our diverging metaphysics makes little difference to what we think is important in life, or to how we behave toward others. If that is the case, why would I want to walk away from my believing interlocutors and join the New Atheists over at their tent, where they are as exclusive in whom they welcome as various groups of religious fundamentalists are about whom they admit to church?

And what does this have to do with Stoicism? One of the things that attracted me to it from the get-go is precisely what others may consider one of its weaknesses: given the Stoic ambiguity over how to interpret the Logos, Stoics can build a very large tent indeed, welcoming everyone from atheists to agnostics, from pantheists and panentheists to theists, as long as none of these guests impose their own metaphysical views on the others. Are you a Christian, or Muslim, or practicing Jew? Fine, you can treat the Logos as a central attribute of a personal God who created the universe. Does your metaphysical preference lean more toward the idea that God is everywhere, to be identified with Nature itself? Then you will feel at home with many of the original Stoics and their conception of the rational principle of the universe. Are you instead an agnostic or atheist? If so, the Logos represents the indisputable *fact* that the cosmos really is organized rationally, even though we still do not know how such organization came about, whether by design or as a result of brute cause and effect. If this were not the case, then logic, mathematics, and science itself would go out the window, and you do believe in them, right?

Mind you, this is no counsel for laziness of mind, or for a politically correct and bland mix of otherwise incompatible positions. It is simply the realization that what is important in life is to live it well, and that such an objective—the eudaimonic existence sought by the ancients—depends very little on whether there is a God or not, and if there is one, on what its specific attributes may or may not be. Besides, as Cicero wisely put it: "There are many questions in philosophy to which no satisfactory answer has yet been given. But the question of the nature of the gods is the darkest and most difficult of all. . . . So various and so contradictory are the opinions of the most learned men on this matter as to persuade one of the truth of the saying that philosophy is the child of ignorance." This was true two millennia ago, and despite what you may have heard of late, it is still true today. So why don't we agree to disagree on this particular matter, and get on together with the serious business of living a good life?

PART II

THE DISCIPLINE OF ACTION: HOW TO BEHAVE IN THE WORLD

Chapter 7

It's All About Character (and Virtue)

Of one thing beware, O man: see what is the price at which you sell your will. If you do nothing else, do not sell your will cheap.

—Epictetus, *Discourses*, I.2

THE OTHER NIGHT EPICTETUS RECOUNTED ONE OF HIS FA-vorite anecdotes, one he regularly uses to make a broader philosophical point. The story concerns Helvidius Priscus, a Roman statesman (and Stoic philosopher, as it turns out) who had the unusual stamina—and luck, until it ran out—to live under several emperors, from Nero to Galba, Otho, Vitellius, and finally Vespasian. According to our friend and guide, "When Vespasian sent to him not to come into the Senate he answered, 'You can forbid me to be a senator; but as long as I am a senator I must come in.' 'Come in then,' he says, 'and be silent.' 'Question me not and I will be silent.' 'But I am bound to question you.' 'And I am bound to say what seems right to me.' 'But, if you say it, I shall kill you.' 'When did I tell you that I was immortal? You will do your part, and I mine. It is yours to kill, mine to die without quailing: yours to banish, mine to go into exile without groaning.' What good, you ask, did Priscus do, being but one? What good does the purple do to the garment? Just this, that being purple it gives distinction and stands out as a fine example to the rest."

Predictably, Vespasian acted on his threat, Priscus was banished from Rome (for the second time in his life), and soon afterwards he was murdered on the order of the emperor. The question rhetorically asked by Epictetus, "What good did Priscus do, being but one?" is as obvious as it is difficult to answer. In the case of the Roman senator, apparently no good came out of this encounter. He was an ardent Republican who refused to recognize Vespasian as emperor, but the Republican cause had by then been lost forever, and Priscus's death caused others to suffer: his wife Fannia commissioned Herennius Senecio (who was part of the Stoic opposition to a later Flavian emperor, Domitian) to write a panegyric in honor of her slain husband, as a result of which Senecio too was put to death. And yet Epictetus had a point when he said that these episodes of human courage and honor "give distinction and stand out as a fine example to the rest." That is why we are still in awe of individuals like Helvidius Priscus almost two millennia after his self-sacrifice.

There are plenty of later and even contemporary stories that could be told by a modern Epictetus to philosophy students; the names of their protagonists and the details of what happened would be different, but these stories would provide equally good examples of how human nature has not changed a bit since Roman times, for better and for worse. One such example is Malala Yousafzai. Her story is well known, but it is worth recalling. Malala was eleven years old when she anonymously began writing a BBC blog detailing the harshly regressive approach of the Taliban toward women's education in the Swat Valley region of Pakistan, where her family ran a chain of schools. Malala was then featured in a *New York Times* documentary, which caused both her initial rise to fame and her targeting by the Taliban. On October 9, 2012, a coward boarded her school bus, asked for her by name, and shot her three times. Amazingly, Malala survived the ordeal, eventually making a full recovery.

That experience alone would have been enough to put her on the same level as Priscus and so many others over the centuries and across cultures who have dared to stand up to repression and barbarism. But it turns out that the shooting was just the beginning for Malala. Despite further threats by the Taliban against her and her father Ziauddin, she has continued to argue publicly and vociferously on behalf of young girls' education, and her activism has been credited with helping to pass Pakistan's first Right to Education Bill. In 2014, at age seventeen, she became the youngest person ever to receive a Nobel Prize, for peace. I am confident that she will keep up the struggle throughout what I hope will be a long and eudaimonic life. Did Malala make a difference? Yes, both in practice (in that respect she was luckier than Priscus) and as a role model for others—"a fine example to the rest" indeed.

But this chapter isn't about role models (we'll get there soon, since they do play a very important part in Stoicism), but rather about the importance of character and the related concept of virtue. Nowadays both words immediately conjure up the sharp divide, especially in the United States, between the right and left sides of the political spectrum.

Conservatives tend to talk a lot about both character and virtue, even when they do not actually practice the latter, while liberals reflexively treat their valorization as thinly disguised tools of oppression. Moreover, it is difficult, after two millennia of Christianity, not to confuse the Christian meaning of "virtue" with the Greco-Roman one that preceded and inspired it. Nonetheless, making that distinction is important and will allow us to go back to conceptions of both character and virtue that supersede political differences, I think, and that both conservatives and liberals can live with—indeed, *should* live with if they really care about the values they claim to care about.

Let's begin by fleshing out the earlier introduction to the four Stoic cardinal virtues and their relation to the modern, Christian-inspired versions. We will then see empirical evidence that these virtues, or at least a very similar set of desirable character traits—which is what virtues are—have been remarkably consistent across a number of time periods and cultures. If nothing else, this reinforces the idea that we are dealing with something truly important for humanity as a cultured social species.

The Stoics derived their understanding of virtue from Socrates, who believed that all virtues are actually different aspects of the same underlying feature: wisdom. The reason why wisdom is the "chief good," according to Socrates, is rather simple: it is the only human ability that is good under every and all circumstances. One can easily imagine other desirable things that are only good under a certain set of circumstances and that can, or even should, be traded off if the circumstances change. To be sure, being wealthy is better than being poor, being healthy is better than being sick, and being educated is better than being ignorant (standard pairs of preferred and dispreferred indifferents). But we also need to know how to deal with all of them. In other words, we must have wisdom—the ability to navigate well the diverse, complex, and often contradictory circumstances of our lives.

The Stoics adopted Socrates's classification of four aspects of virtue, which they thought of as four tightly interlinked character traits: (practical) wisdom, courage, temperance, and justice. Practical wisdom allows us to make decisions that improve our *eudaimonia*, the (ethically) good life. Courage can be physical, but more broadly refers to the moral aspect—for instance, the ability to act well under challenging circumstances, as Priscus and Malala did. Temperance makes it possible for us to control our desires and actions so that we don't yield to excesses. Justice, for Socrates and the Stoics, refers not to an abstract theory of how society should be run, but rather to the practice of treating other human beings with dignity and fairness.

One crucial feature of the Stoic (and Socratic) conception of virtue is that the different virtues cannot be practiced independently: one cannot be both intemperate and courageous, in the Stoic-Socratic meaning of the term. Although it makes perfect sense for us to say that, for instance, an individual has shown courage in battle and yet regularly drinks to excess or is ill-tempered, for the Stoics that person would not be virtuous, because virtue is an all-or-nothing package. I never said Stoic philosophy isn't demanding.

What did the Christians do with the Socratic package of virtues? They took it on board wholesale and expanded it.

Thomas Aquinas, one of the most influential Christian theologians of all time, developed the notion of "heavenly virtues" in his *Summa Theologiae*, published in 1273. Basically, Aquinas kept the four Stoic virtues and added three peculiarly Christian ones, originally proposed by Paul of Tarsus: faith, hope, and charity. Aquinas's system thus featured four cardinal virtues and three so-called transcendent ones, and he organized the resulting seven hierarchically: wisdom was the most important of the cardinal virtues (as it was for Socrates), but all four are placed below the transcendental virtues, among which charity sits on top.

Other cultures have developed, more or less independently, their own sets of virtues as socially important character traits, each arriving at its own classification of the relations among virtues. Interestingly, though, there is much more convergence than we would expect in these days when cultural relativism is so often portrayed as the norm. A study by Katherine Dahlsgaard, Christopher Peterson, and Martin Seligman looked at how virtue is articulated in Buddhism, Christianity, Confucianism, Hinduism, Judaism, Taoism, and what they call "Athenian philosophy" (mostly Socrates, Plato, and Aristotle). They found a rather surprising amount of congruence among all of these religious-philosophical traditions and identified a set of six "core" virtues:

> *Courage:* Emotional strengths that involve the exercise of will to accomplish goals in the face of opposition, external or internal; examples include bravery, perseverance, and authenticity (honesty).

Justice: Civic strengths that underlie healthy community life; examples include fairness, leadership, and citizenship or teamwork.

Humanity: Interpersonal strengths that involve "tending and befriending" others; examples include love and kindness.

Temperance: Strengths that protect against excess; examples include forgiveness, humility, prudence, and self-control.

Wisdom: Cognitive strengths that entail the acquisition and use of knowledge; examples include creativity, curiosity, judgment, and perspective (providing counsel to others).

Transcendence: Strengths that forge connections to the larger universe and thereby provide meaning; examples include gratitude, hope, and spirituality.

Four of the six are indistinguishable from the Stoic virtues. Stoics also accepted the importance of "humanity" and "transcendence," although they didn't think of these as virtues, but rather as attitudes toward others (humanity) and toward the universe at large (transcendence). The Stoic version of humanity is embedded in their concept of *oikeiôsis* and Hierocles's contracting circles of concern, which are at the center of the Cynic-Stoic concept of cosmopolitanism: the idea that we ought to extend the sympathy we have for kin to our friends, acquaintances, fellow countrymen, and beyond to humanity at large (and even, some Stoics hinted, to the suffering of sentient animals).

As for transcendence, the Stoic Logos entails a sense of perspective about our relationship with the cosmos and our place in it. Here is one of my favorite examples, a meditation that Marcus Aurelius reminded himself to engage in regularly: "The Pythagoreans bid us in the morning look to the heavens that we may be reminded of those bodies that continually do the same things and in the same manner perform their work, and also be reminded of their purity and nudity. For there is no veil over a star." I love the poetry of that last sentence, and I have been doing the early morning meditation from different parts of the world during my travels, always finding it a soothing experience and a salutary reminder of the large universe that we inhabit and often neglect to think of while we go about our busy daily lives.

Returning to the virtues, the broader point here is not that Stoicism somehow got it right while other traditions did not, but rather that human societies that have developed philosophies of life have repeatedly come up with remarkably similar lists of what we call virtues. I do not want to speculate on whether such convergence is rooted in the earlier biological evolution of humanity, though it is clear from studies in comparative primatology that we share with other species of primates a number of prosocial behaviors that we tend to call "moral." Dahlsgaard and her colleagues also point out in passing that results similar to their own have emerged from the few existing studies of virtues in nonliterate societies—for instance, the Inughuit of northern Greenland and the Maasai of western Kenya. Whether it is biology, culture, or, more likely, a combination of both, the fact is that very disparate human societies, rooted in very distinct religious-philosophical traditions, all seem to value the same core group of character traits in their members, and these are the very same traits and attitudes that Stoics have been teaching about for more than two millennia.

I mentioned earlier that how one reacts to the word "character" these days has become a quick litmus test for whether one's outlook is politically conservative or liberal, with conservatives insisting that we should go back to emphasizing character in schools, families, and the country at large, and liberals rejecting such talk as a not-so-subtle attempt to maintain white male privilege, patriarchy, and the like. This, I think, is highly unfortunate. Given evidence of the universality of valuing character across human cultures, there is no reason why the concept should have become associated with just one side of the political spectrum in contemporary Western discourse. Epictetus and other ancients saw character as both evolving throughout human psychological development and fundamental to our personal identity: "'Lay aside the senator's dress, and put on rags and appear in that character.' Very well: is it not given me still to display a noble voice? In what part then do you appear now?" Epictetus is reminding us that whatever we don in the course of the day, the toga of a senator, the suit of someone working on Wall Street, or the stereotypical tweed jacket with elbow patches of a university professor, the true value of a person lies in their core, and that core—our character—remains regardless of the role we happen to play in society, whether by choice, happenstance, or necessity.

That is why it is crucial to social life not only to work to improve your own character but to be able to assess the character of other people. There is a good story in this regard concerning Diogenes the Cynic. One day (presumably before he turned full-time philosopher, when he was still a banker, of all things), he was asked for a letter of introduction. He told his interlocutor: "You are a man, and that his eyes will tell him; but whether you are good or bad he will discover, if he has skill to distinguish the good from the bad; and if he has not that skill, he will never discover it, though I should write him ten thousand letters." Epictetus further clarified this point for my benefit: "A drachma might just as well ask to be introduced to someone in order to be tested. If the man is a judge of silver, you will introduce yourself. We ought, therefore, to have some faculty to guide us in life, as the assayer has in dealing with silver, that I may be able to say as he does, 'Give me any drachma you please, and I will distinguish.'" In other words, your character is your best calling card, and if you interact with good judges of character, that's all you'll need.

I thought of this while watching the 2016 presidential primaries unfolding in the United States, which happened to take place at about the same time as the local elections in Italy, including that for mayor of Rome. The similarities between the two countries' elections were both striking and disheartening. What seemed pretty obvious to me was that Diogenes would have found most (though not necessarily all) of the major candidates—across the political spectrum and in both countries—obviously deficient in character. Okay, maybe the standards of the Cynics were impossibly high for most human beings, but still, the gulf between the lofty ideal and the stark reality looked to me like a wide chasm, and one far too ample for comfort considering that some of these people were actually going to win the elections, and one of them was going to become the president of the most powerful nation on earth.

To be fair, it is not easy to judge someone's character if we have not met him personally and have no history of repeated interactions. But when it comes to highly visible public figures, modern media allow us to glean important clues from what they say, how they say it, and especially how they act. By those standards, I detected little in the way of courage or temperance, mostly vague gestures toward justice, and remarkably little practical wisdom—arguably the most important of the virtues—among these candidates.

Character takes on a predictable role in politics, with conservatives emphasizing the character of their candidates at the expense of specific programmatic platforms, while liberals do the exact reverse. But in politics as in everyday life, there is no sharp separation between the two: I certainly want to know the general ideas of a given presidential candidate, or mayoral candidate, about crucial issues that he is likely to face should he win the election. What is his take on climate change, foreign affairs, political and economic inequality, individual rights, and so forth? But it is also obvious that once in office he will have to deal with whatever complex political, economic, and social landscape Fate thrusts upon him, and navigating that landscape successfully will require more than some general ideas of where to go, as theoretically sound as they may be. Indeed, what will be needed are exactly the fundamental virtues: the courage to do the right thing under difficult circumstances, the temperance to rein in excesses, a sense of justice in considering how people are going to be affected by his decisions, and of course the practical wisdom that will allow him to negotiate treacherous and always -changing waters.

Epictetus used an apt seafaring metaphor to make a related point:

> For the helmsman to wreck his vessel, he does not need the same resources, as he needs to save it: if he turn it but a little too far to the wind, he is lost; yes, and if he do it not deliberately but from mere want of attention, he is lost all the same. It is very much the same in life: if you doze but a little, all that you have amassed up till now leaves you. Keep awake then and watch your impressions: it is no trifle you have in keeping, but self-respect, honor, constancy, a quiet mind, untouched by distress, or fear, or agitation— in a word, freedom. What are you going to sell all this for? Look and see what your purchase is worth.

Both public figures and every single one of us need to cultivate virtue and character, but we also need to remain vigilant in order not to derail the ship we command, be it an entire country or our own private lives, as even an apparently inconsequential, momentary distraction can be disastrous. And above all, we need to be cognizant of what our integrity is worth: if we decide to sell it, it shouldn't be for cheap. It is hard to read those words and not think about political scandals and corruption, but perhaps the cleanup should start closer to home, with our own behavior, our own too-often-unacknowledged propensity to compromise principles for the sake of convenience, our lack of courage when it is called for, our mostly theoretical sense of justice, our often flaunted temperance, and our own manifestly very limited wisdom in managing whatever life happens to throw at us.

Chapter 8

A Very Crucial Word

> For if one shows this, a man will retire from his error of
> himself; but as long as you do not succeed in showing this,
> you need not wonder if he persists in his error, for he acts
> because he has an impression that he is right.

—Epictetus, *Discourses*, II.26

Not so long ago I went down to the Ghione, one of
the many small theaters scattered throughout the quarters of
old Rome. The show was a production of *Medea,* the classic
tragedy by Euripides, first performed in Athens at the Di-
onysia festival in 431 BCE. Back then, the premiere didn't go
well, and Euripides placed last in that year's competition. But
he certainly had the last laugh. Unlike his rival Euphorion's
work, which won then but has since been largely forgotten,
Medea has been the most frequently staged Greek tragedy
throughout the last century.

The night I went, the wonderful Italian actress Barbara
De Rossi was playing the title role. Playing Medea is a very
difficult undertaking because the actress needs to somehow
evoke a feeling of sympathy for a character who, after all, kills

her own children in revenge against her husband Jason (he of the Argonauts), who has just left her for a local princess. By the end of the play, the chorus is so shocked (and certainly so was the original public in Athens) that it simply cannot make sense of what has just unfolded onstage:

> *Manifold are thy shapings, Providence!*
> *Many a hopeless matter gods arrange.*
> *What we expected never came to pass,*
> *What we did not expect the gods brought to bear;*
> *So have things gone, this whole experience through!*

De Rossi pulled it off very nicely, but of course a lot of the credit goes to Euripides's brilliant study in the strong, inter-twined human emotions of love and hatred. You see, Medea had previously helped Jason steal the fabled Golden Fleece from her native land, in the process betraying her father and killing her brother. She did it for love and also to escape her "barbarian" country and come to civilized Greece (remember, the play was written by a Greek). One of the intriguing characteristics of the piece is that it can be (and has been) read either as a tale of misogyny and xenophobia (Medea is a woman *and* a barbarian) or as a proto-feminist story of a woman's struggle in a patriarchal society.

The violent passions of Medea may seem to be very much at odds with the alleged detachment advocated by the Stoics. Nevertheless, Epictetus relies on the story to make some cru-cial points about human nature and the practice of philosophy. It will take us a little bit to get back to Medea, so hang on tight.

As it happens, Epictetus encountered the same problem that I run up against with my own students: they really want to study philosophy, but their parents tell them that it isn't practical, it's a waste of time, and the like. Epictetus said: "This is the defense that we must plead with parents who are angered at their children studying philosophy: 'Suppose I am in error, my father, and ignorant of what is fitting and proper for me. If, then, this cannot be taught or learnt, why do you reproach me? If it can be taught, teach me, and, if you cannot, let me learn from those who say that they know. For what think you? That I fall into evil and fail to do well because I wish to?'" I pointed out to him that such talk is well and good, but it doesn't really get to the heart of the matter, which is not just to *claim* that learning philosophy will make you a better person, but to convincingly *show* that it does.

So Epictetus continued: "What is the reason that we assent to a thing? Because it seems to us that it is so. It is impossible that we shall assent to that which seems not to be. Why? Because this is the nature of the mind—to agree to what is true, and disagree with what is false, and withhold judgment on what is doubtful." Maybe, I replied, but an actual example would be more convincing to me, and especially to my students' parents. "Feel now, if you can, that it is night. It is impossible. Put away the feeling that it is day. It is impossible. . . . When a man assents, then, to what is false, know that he had no wish to assent to the false: 'for no soul is robbed of the truth with its own consent,' as Plato says, but the false seemed to him true." Well, that's intriguing, isn't it? The point is that nobody errs on purpose. Whatever we do, we think it is the right thing to do, according to whatever criterion we have developed or adopted to establish right action.

Much more recently, the philosopher Hannah Arendt made a similar point with her controversial idea of the "banality of evil." Arendt was sent by *The New Yorker* to cover the trial of Adolf Eichmann, an SS-Obersturmbannführer (lieutenant colonel) who had been one of the high-ranking Nazi officers in charge of the logistics of Hitler's so-called Final Solution for the Jewish people. Arendt wrote a series of highly controversial articles for the magazine about the trial, and these were eventually collected and published in her landmark book *Eichmann in Jerusalem: A Report on the Banality of Evil*.

Part of the controversy hinged on the idea Arendt developed that "evil" is often the result of lack of thought, meaning that people usually don't *want* to do evil, and certainly don't think of themselves as evildoers. But they also tend to follow the general opinion without critical analysis, and indeed— as in Eichmann's case—they are often convinced that they are doing a good job. The Obersturmbannführer was proud of the efficiency with which he worked, never mind that the work resulted in the deaths of hundreds of thousands of innocents in Hungary, where his activities took place.

I found a tape of the last interview given by Arendt, who further clarified her thinking about the banality of evil (some alternative translations of key German words are in brackets):

> During the war, Ernst Jünger came across some peasants, and a farmer had taken in Russian prisoners of war straight from the camps, and naturally they were completely starving—you know how Russian prisoners of war were treated

here. And [the farmer] says to Jünger, "Well, they're sub-human, just like cattle—look how they devour food like cattle." Jünger comments on this story, "It's sometimes as if the German people were being possessed by the Devil." And he didn't mean anything "demonic" by that. You see, there's something outrageously stupid [*dumm* = ignorant, unwise] about this story. I mean the story is stupid, so to speak. The man doesn't see that this is just what starving people do, right? And anyone would behave like that. But there's something really outrageous [*empörend* = shocking, revolting] about this stupidity. . . . Eichmann was perfectly intelligent, but in this respect he had this sort of stupidity [*Dummheit* = irrationality, senselessness]. It was this stupidity that was so outrageous. And that was what I actually meant by banality. There's nothing deep about it [the ignorance]—nothing demonic! There's simply the reluctance ever to imagine what the other person is experiencing, correct?

What both Arendt and Epictetus are getting at is a crucial Stoic concept, one that originally derives from Socrates: people don't do "evil" on purpose, they do it out of "ignorance." Whenever I say this, someone is guaranteed to get outraged. What? Do I seriously mean to say that Hitler wasn't evil? How could I possibly be so naive? Or perhaps I harbor questionable sympathies? But as with many terms in philosophy, "evil" and "ignorance" don't mean quite what we expect.

The term "evil" simply seems to invoke an unnecessary metaphysical category. If what we are doing is simply labeling a particularly nasty type of bad behavior, then there is little problem. But not infrequently, when we talk of evil, we slide into a fallacy known as "reification" (literally, making a thing), which means speaking of a concept as if it has some kind of mind-independent existence, as if it is in some sense "out there." Take the phrase "evil personified," as in "Hitler was evil personified," meaning the embodiment, the physical incarnation, of evil. But "evil" isn't a thing characterized by independent existence. It has no metaphysical consistency: it is simply a shorthand for the really, really bad stuff that people do, or for the really, really bad character that leads people to do said stuff. So, in an important philosophical sense, "evil" doesn't exist (but the really, really bad stuff does!).

Now let us tackle the more difficult concept—the idea that people do evil (in this nonmetaphysical sense) out of "ignorance." In the *Euthydemus* dialogue, Plato has Socrates say, "Wisdom alone, is the good for man, ignorance the only evil," a phrase that has been misunderstood ever since. The word used by Plato is *amathia*, which, to be precise, does not mean "ignorance," as it turns out. The philosopher Sherwood Belangia has written extensively on this topic, and it is well worth considering his explanation of it.

Belangia begins with a conversation (from Plato's dialogue *Alcibiades Major*) between Socrates and his friend Alcibiades, an Athenian general and politician with, shall we say, a more than checkered record, from an ethical point of view:

> SOCRATES: But if you are bewildered, is it not clear from what has gone before that you are not only ignorant of the greatest things, but while not knowing them you think that you do?

ALCIBIADES: I am afraid so.

SOCRATES: Alack then, Alcibiades, for the plight you are in! I shrink indeed from giving it a name, but still, as we are alone, let me speak out. You are wedded to stupidity, my fine friend, of the vilest kind; you are impeached of this by your own words, out of your own mouth; and this, it seems, is why you dash into politics before you have been educated. And you are not alone in this plight, but you share it with most of those who manage our city's affairs, except just a few, and perhaps your guardian, Pericles.

The two Greek words for "ignorance" and "stupidity" are, respectively, *agnoia* and *amathia*. Among Athenians, Alcibiades was one of the most educated—in the normal sense of the word—and he was obviously intelligent, again in the normal sense. So neither of the English words "ignorance" nor "stupidity" really describe what Socrates is getting at. Instead, Alcibiades is unwise: he "dashes into politics" without the proper "education," meaning without the sort of wisdom that comes from being virtuous. The contrast that Socrates makes between his friend and Pericles is particularly illuminating: Pericles was an Athenian orator famous for being not just educated and smart, but also wise. That is what made him a good politician, and that is what—tragically, as it turns out—was missing in Alcibiades. *Amathia*, then, can best be thought of as lack of wisdom—the opposite of *sophia*, the word that gives root to "philosophy."

Belangia helpfully adds: "A-gnoia means literally 'not-knowing'; a-mathia means literally 'not-learning.' In addition to the type of *amathia* that is an inability to learn, there is another form that is an unwillingness to learn. . . . Robert Musil in an essay called On Stupidity, distinguished between two forms of stupidity, one he called 'an honorable kind' due to a lack of natural ability and another, much more sinister kind, that he called 'intelligent stupidity.'"

Belangia also quotes philosopher Glenn Hughes, who provided a further elucidation of the concept of *amathia* and connected it to Nazi Germany. To Hughes, "intelligent stupidity" was not "so much lack of intelligence as failure of intelligence, for the reason that it presumes to accomplishments to which it has no right." Intelligent stupidity "is no mental illness, yet it is most lethal; a dangerous disease of the mind that endangers life itself." The danger lies "not in an inability to understand but in a refusal to understand, [and] any healing or reversal of it will not occur through rational argumentation, through a greater accumulation of data and knowledge, or through experiencing new and different feelings." Instead, intelligent stupidity is a "spiritual sickness," and in need of a spiritual cure.

So *amathia* seems to be a crucial word missing from the English vocabulary. It is the opposite of wisdom, a kind of dis-knowledge of how to deal with other human beings, and it results in awful actions undertaken by otherwise perfectly functional, intelligent human beings. Moreover, people characterized by *amathia* cannot simply be persuaded by reasoned argument, because they understand the argument but are crucially deficient in their character, which, as the Stoics have shown us, is developed over time by a combination of instincts, environmental influences (especially family guidance), and reason. If something goes wrong early on in a person's development, it is difficult for reason alone to rectify the resulting *amathia* later in life.

Which finally brings us back to Medea. Epictetus reminded me of what Euripides has Medea say:

> *I know full well what ills I mean to do*
> *But passion overpowers what counsel bids me.*

Epictetus added: "Here the very gratification of passion and the vengeance she takes on her husband she believes to be more to her profit than saving her children." Yes, I replied, but she is obviously deceived. "Why then are you indignant with her, because, unhappy woman, she is deluded on the greatest matters and is transformed from a human being into a serpent? Why do you not rather pity her—if so it may be? As we pity the blind and the lame, so should we pity those who are blinded and lamed in their most sovereign faculties. The man who remembers this, I say, will be angry with no one, indignant with no one, revile none, blame none, hate none, offend none."

This is a stunning and profound insight into the human condition. It also shows a degree of compassion that popular lore associates far more with, say, Christianity than with Stoicism. And yet this is Epictetus, the slave-turned-teacher, who is speaking. Medea knew it was wrong to make her children suffer to punish Jason, but emotion (vengeance), not reason, drove her to act as she did. Epictetus advises pity, not indignation or anger, as our proper attitude toward Medea because she is not "evil," whatever that may mean, but a person lacking something important, like a lame person (the same word Epictetus uses to describe his own condition). Specifically, Medea lacks wisdom and is affected by *amathia*, the sort of dis-knowledge that brings ordinary people to make unreasonable judgments about certain situations that then lead them to what outsiders correctly perceive as horrible acts. If we internalize this Stoic attitude—or its equivalent in Buddhism or Christianity—we indeed will be angry or indignant with no one; there will be no one we revile, blame, hate, or are offended by. I submit that the resulting world would be significantly better than the one we currently live in.

Epictetus elaborated on why he thought people like Medea are such tragic figures:

> Every error implies conflict; for since he who errs does not wish to go wrong but to go right, plainly he is not doing what he wishes. For what does the thief wish to do? What is to his interest. If then thieving is against his interest, he is not doing what he wishes. But every rational soul by nature dislikes conflict; and so, as long as a man does not understand that he is in conflict, there is nothing to prevent him from doing conflicting acts, but, whenever he understands, strong necessity makes him abandon the conflict and avoid it.

That is, Medea did not wish to err, but was simply convinced that she was doing the right thing. The same, I'm sure Epictetus would argue, was true for Eichmann, despite the vast differences between him and Medea in circumstances, apparent reasons for acting, and ultimate outcomes.

Modern psychologists have discovered a pertinent phenomenon known as cognitive dissonance, a condition first described by the psychologist Leon Festinger. Cognitive dissonance is a very uncomfortable psychological state that occurs when someone becomes aware of the conflict between two judgments that he holds to be equally true. People do not want to experience cognitive dissonance, just as Epictetus said that people do not want to knowingly be in error. Thus, they reduce dissonance by endorsing any explanation that deploys what they think are good reasons leading to sound judgments, even though to others those reasons and judgments appear to be obvious and even absurd rationalizations. Aesop described this delightfully in his famous fable about the fox and the grapes, back in the sixth century BCE.

The uncomfortable truth is, again, that people suffering from cognitive dissonance are neither stupid nor ignorant. I have encountered plenty of smart and well-educated individuals who nonetheless reject Darwin's theory of evolution, one of the most firmly established scientific theories ever. They *have* to reject it, because it seems to them to be in irreconcilable conflict with the Bible, the reference point for their whole lives as devout Christians. If we arrive at the judgment that *either* Darwin is right *or* the word of God is true, then it is perfectly natural—rational even—for some of us to choose God over Darwin. Epictetus would not have been surprised, and neither should I have been when I met fundamentalist creationists face to face for the first time. But I was much younger (and somewhat less wise?) then. As the writer

Michael Shermer has observed, the more clever people are, the better they are at rationalizing away the sources of their cognitive dissonance. Conspiracy theorists, for instance, are often brilliant at explaining what others perceive as gaping holes in their theories of how the world *really* works.

What's to be done then? Once more, psychological research may be helpful here. We know that the best way to help students change their conceptual outlook about scientific notions is to purposefully *increase* their cognitive dissonance until they feel so uncomfortable that they themselves seek out more information and new sources to resolve the conflict. This, of course, is not always possible—I doubt that it would have worked with Medea or Eichmann—but the notion provides us with a good understanding of both what is going on and what, if anything, can be done about it.

Still, I worry about the same sort of thing that critics of Hannah Arendt worried about: isn't the idea of evil being banal, of *amathia*, dangerously close to an excuse for horrific behavior? Doesn't it, at the very least, encourage us to respond passively to "evil"? Naturally, Epictetus had pondered this as well: "'Such a one reviled you.' Many thanks to him for not striking. 'But he did strike too.' Many thanks to him for not wounding. 'But he did wound.' Many thanks to him for not killing. For when, or in whose school, did he learn 'that man is a gentle and sociable creature and that wrongdoing in itself does great harm to the wrongdoer'? If, then, he has not learnt this or been convinced of it, why should he not follow what appears to be his interest?"

If this doesn't sound to you like "turn the other cheek," I don't know what does. But Epictetus didn't stop at counseling endurance and patience, although he certainly did that too: he actually diagnosed what is going amiss: The wrongdoer does not understand that he is doing harm to himself first and foremost, because he suffers from *amathia*, lack of knowledge of what is truly good for himself. And what is good for him is the same thing that is good for all human beings, according to the Stoics: applying reason to improve social living.

As far as the rest of us are concerned, remembering that people do bad things out of lack of wisdom is not only a reminder to be compassionate toward others, it also constantly tells us just how important it is to develop wisdom.

CHAPTER 9

THE ROLE OF ROLE MODELS

What would Heracles have been if he had said, "How am I to prevent a big lion from appearing, or a big boar, or brutal men?" What care you, I say? If a big boar appears, you will have a greater struggle to engage in; if evil men appear, you will free the world from evil men.

—EPICTETUS, *DISCOURSES*, IV.10

ON OCTOBER 13, 1992, I WAS WATCHING THE VICE PRESIDENtial debate of the American electoral season. I had moved to the United States from Rome a couple of years earlier, and the whole idea of televised debates as "infotainment" was very new to me. There were three men onstage: Al Gore and Dan Quayle, two career politicians, and an awkward guy named James Stockdale. It was not a good night for Stockdale, who began the debate with the amusing statement, "Who am I? Why am I here?" People initially took his remarks as endearingly self-deprecating, but then he quickly showed that he really had very little clue as to what he was doing there. He seemed foolish, but little did I know that Stockdale would become one of my role models, several decades after that night and about ten years after his death. Stockdale, you see, was a modern Stoic, and one whose story is well worth telling.

To do so, we have to go back to September 9, 1965. American involvement in the Vietnam War had started in earnest the year before, after the bizarre "incident" of the Tonkin Gulf: American warships fired at nothing in the middle of the night, and President Lyndon Johnson used that as the official excuse to begin "retaliatory" bombing raids on North Vietnam. Hearing the news, Stockdale, who was commander of Fighter Squadron 51 of the US Navy and who had actually been at Tonkin, commented, "Retaliation for what?" He was ordered to keep silent.

On September 9, Stockdale was flying over North Vietnam when he was shot down and captured. He would spend seven and a half years in the so-called Hanoi Hilton, enduring an ordeal that included beatings and torture, as well as being regularly locked up in leg irons and confined to a three-by-nine-foot cell without windows. Despite these incredibly trying circumstances, Stockdale managed to organize his fellow prisoners, creating and enforcing a code of conduct to regulate their behavior. Moreover, in order not to be used for propaganda by the North Vietnamese, he first slit his scalp with a razor, to disfigure himself, and when that didn't work he proceeded to bash his face with a stool to make it swollen and himself useless to the enemy. At one point he even slit his wrists to avoid being tortured and revealing the underground activities of his comrades. Eventually Stockdale was released and came back to the United States, in horrible physical condition. He began to recover, however, and in 1976 he was awarded the Medal of Honor, the highest military recognition, given for acts of valor above and beyond the call of duty.

When he was asked in an interview who didn't make it out of the Hanoi Hilton, Stockdale replied:

> Oh, that's easy, the optimists. Oh, they were the ones who said, "We're going to be out by Christmas." And Christmas would come, and Christmas would go. Then they'd say, "We're going to be out by Easter." And Easter would come, and Easter would go. And then Thanksgiving, and then it would be Christmas again. And they died of a broken heart. . . . This is a very important lesson. You must never confuse faith that you will prevail in the end— which you can never afford to lose—with the discipline to confront the most brutal facts of your current reality, whatever they might be.

The interviewer referred to this as the Stockdale Paradox, but he might as well have attributed it to the original source: Epictetus. Stockdale, back in 1959, had been sent by the Navy to study at Stanford University in pursuit of a master's degree in international relations and—of all things—comparative Marxist thought. Finding himself rather bored with his regular studies, he wandered into the Philosophy Department. There he met Prof. Phil Rhinelander, who changed Stockdale's life profoundly. The Navy student enrolled in Rhinelander's two-term course, "The Problems of Good and Evil," midway through the first term. To make up for the delay, the professor offered Stockdale one-on-one tutoring in his office, to catch up with the other students. In their last session,

Rhinelander picked up a copy of Epictetus's *Handbook* and gave it to Stockdale, saying: "As a military man, I think you'll have special interest in this. Frederick the Great never went on a campaign without a copy of this handbook in his kit." Stockdale eventually read both the *Handbook* and the *Discourses* many times, and he later credited Epictetus with saving his life in Vietnam by giving him the moral strength to overcome his ordeal, as well as the rational lucidity to see what could and could not be done about it. It was a terrible application of the Stoic dichotomy of control. In 1981 Stockdale became a fellow of the Hoover Institution, based at Stanford, and for twelve years there he wrote and lectured extensively about Stoicism.

Nothing of what you are about to read should be construed as either a defense of the American intervention in Vietnam (which Stockdale knew was based on a lie) or an attempt to demonize the North Vietnamese. It is only a personal human story that we all ought to reflect on. Stockdale understood an important truth about war that applies to life in general: holding the moral high ground and maintaining self-respect is more important than the facts on the ground, be they the weaponry on each side (in the case of war) or the circumstances of our ordinary lives. Doing so involves a mind game, however, and that is why Stoicism is so useful: it is a major mind game centered on keeping one's moral high ground and self-respect.

The first real test for Stockdale came when he was shot down on that September 9. As he put it: "After ejection I had about 30 seconds to make my last statement in freedom before I landed on the main street of that little village right ahead.

And so help me, I whispered to myself: 'Five years down there at the least. I'm leaving the world of technology and entering the world of Epictetus.'"

As soon as he landed and was captured, Stockdale understood all too well Epictetus's dichotomy of control, specifically concerning his own stature in life. In a matter of minutes, he went from being an admired officer, commanding 100 pilots and over 1,000 men, to "taking the ropes" and being vilified as a criminal. After quickly freeing himself from his parachute, he was surrounded by a dozen men: "By the time the tackling and pummeling and twisting and wrenching were over, and it lasted for three or more minutes before the guy in the pith helmet got there to blow his whistle, I had a very badly broken leg that I felt sure would be with me for life. And that hunch turned out to be right." He later recalled that Epictetus too had been crippled for life after his leg was broken by his first master, and that Epictetus's assessment of that fact had been: "Lameness is an impediment to the leg, but not to the will; and say this to yourself with regard to everything that happens. For you will find it to be an impediment to something else, but not truly to yourself." Stockdale had seven and a half more years to truly appreciate just how right the Greek philosopher was.

By the time he was brought into the Hanoi Hilton, Stockdale had resolved to do precisely what Epictetus advised: to play whatever part Fate had allotted to him to the best of his abilities. He constantly kept in mind that his enemies would win only if he succumbed to two things: fear and loss of self-respect. Stockdale studied his captors, and particularly the man who was in charge of torturing him. As Epictetus and Arendt would both see, had they been there, he came to understand that the man was not evil, but rather that he was doing his job with what he perceived as integrity. Perhaps surprisingly, Stockdale developed not hatred, but respect for him. A torturer's job is to break the prisoner's spirit, to instill fear. Knowing this, Epictetus arrived at the only possible response: "When a man who has set his will neither on dying nor upon living at any cost, comes into the presence of the tyrant, what is there to prevent him from being without fear? Nothing."

Thanks to having internalized Epictetus's philosophy, Stockdale was a man on a mission, even in prison and with a broken leg. He created a secret society of prisoners to whom, as the highest-ranking officer, he would do his best to issue sensible orders to resist the enemy. He gave his soldiers practical advice as to what was and was not permissible to admit under torture. Realizing that the US government's official policy of providing the enemy only with name, rank, serial number, and date of birth would quickly get many of them killed, Stockdale devised alternative guidelines of his own, which included not bowing in public and not admitting to any crime—all designed to thwart the attempts of the North Vietnamese to exploit prisoners for propaganda purposes. Sure enough, the propaganda footage that was put out backfired, since many soldiers used their appearances on film to engage in jokes at the expense of their captors. On one occasion, Nels Tanner, a friend of Stockdale's, answered a request for the names of pilots who had turned in their wings to express opposition to the war by providing two: Lieutenants Clark Kent and Ben Casey. Tanner endured the consequences of his defiance: three successive days of rope torture followed by 123 days in leg stocks and isolation.

Eventually, the North Vietnamese understood the inner workings of the resistance within the American group and sent Stockdale and nine others to solitary confinement for periods ranging from three and a half to more than four years. Another of Stockdale's companions, Howie Rutledge, enrolled in a master's degree program when he finally made it back home and wrote a thesis on whether torture or solitary confinement was more likely to break a person's spirit. To collect his research data he sent out questionnaires to his comrades and to others who had been prisoners of war. The results were striking: those who had spent less than two years in confinement said that torture was the worst; those who had spent more than two years in isolation said that the latter experience trumped even torture. That's because, after going that long without seeing anyone, a person desperately needs friends, quite regardless of who they are, their ideologies, or their politics. Stockdale interpreted Rutledge's finding in the light of Epictetus's teachings—that it is shame, not physical pain, that truly brings down a human being. When he himself emerged from that experience, he remembered that, asked what was going to be the fruit of all his teachings, Epictetus replied: "Tranquillity, fearlessness, and freedom." That certainly came true for James Stockdale.

One important question is whether it was truly Stoicism that made Stockdale invulnerable to torture and solitary confinement, or whether Stoicism was simply an after-the-fact rationalization of feats that resulted from his innate character. A more philosophical way to put this is: can virtue be taught, or are people born with whatever virtue they have? Not only did the ancient Greeks debate this issue in detail, but modern biology and developmental psychology have uncovered a significant amount of empirical evidence that is very relevant to it.

In Plato's *Meno,* Socrates is asked by the character bearing that name: "Can you tell me, Socrates, is human excellence something teachable? Or, if not teachable, is it something to be acquired by training? Or, if it cannot be acquired either by training or by teaching, does it accrue to me at birth or in some other way?" After a lengthy discussion, Socrates concludes that "excellence" (or virtue) *may* be teachable in principle, but as there are no teachers of it to be found anywhere, in practice it is not. The implication, then, is that people who have it probably acquire a propensity for it as an endowment at birth. Aristotle, however, had different ideas. He made a crucial distinction between *moral* virtue and *intellectual* virtue, the former arising from both natural disposition and habit acquired while growing up and the latter resulting from reflection in a mature mind. It follows, then, that there are three sources of virtue: some comes from our natural endowment, some is obtained by habit, especially early in life, and some can be acquired intellectually and therefore can be taught.

This "mixed" model of the acquisition of virtue happens to work well with Stoic philosophy and is also favored by modern research in cognitive psychology. The Stoics, as we have seen, held a developmental model of morality, thinking that we naturally come equipped with the ability to have regard not just for ourselves but also for our caretakers and other people with whom we come into regular contact early on in life. Once the age of reason arrives, however, when we are about seven or eight years old, we can begin to further build our virtuous character by two means: habit and (more so later in life) explicit philosophical reflection.

In modern psychology, perhaps the most famous attempt to summarize how people develop morally is Lawrence Kohlberg's theory of six stages of moral development, which builds on Jean Piaget's original work, as well as on a significant amount of modern empirical evidence. The six stages described by Kohlberg are grouped into three phases: pre-conventional morality (which begins with a stage regulated by obedience and punishment and then moves to a stage of self-orientation), conventional morality (from a stage of interpersonal accord and conformity to one of maintenance of social order and response to authority), and post-conventional morality (from a stage of response to a perceived social contract to one of adherence to universal ethical principles). Kohlberg's theory has been criticized on a number of levels, including too much emphasis on rational decision-making and on the ethical concept of justice (as opposed to, respectively, the role of instinctual judgments and of other ethical virtues, such as care for others). But it does seem to hold fairly well across cultures, even though people go through the different stages at different rates, and distinct cultures emphasize some aspects of the model more than others. Regardless, we do not have to buy into a specific modern theory of moral-psychological development to agree with the general idea that we get our ethics from a combination of instincts, training, and—for those so inclined—explicit critical reflection. This theory is in accord with repeated findings by biologists who study gene-environment interactions in a variety of living organisms: complex traits, especially behavioral ones, seem almost always to develop through a continuous feedback of genes and environments, nature intermingled with nurture. And of course, for human beings a major aspect of the environment is our culture and our social interactions with other members of our species. Which is all we need to get back to Stoicism.

Role models such as James Stockdale, Paconius Agrippinus, Helvidius Priscus, and Malala Yousafzai highlight the point that Stoicism is a practical philosophy, not abstract theorizing. While Stoics of course put forth ethical principles for how to conduct ourselves and live the eudaimonic life, their emphasis was on how real people behave, not just how they talk. Observing and imitating role models, then, is one powerful way to work on our own virtue. We do something like this in modern societies as well, whenever we hold up public figures as examples to our younger generations. The problem nowadays is that, by and large, we do a pretty bad job of picking role models. We glorify actors, singers, athletes, and generic "celebrities," only to be disappointed when—predictably—it turns out that their excellence at reciting, singing, playing basketball, or racking up Facebook likes and Twitter followers has pretty much nothing to do with their moral fiber.

A similar problem arises with the contemporary, highly inflated use of the word "hero," especially in the United States. Some brave people who are willing to sacrifice themselves for the common good truly deserve that appellative (though they don't have to be almost exclusively drawn from the ranks of the military or the police). But someone who dies, say, as a result of a terrorist attack is not a hero—he is a victim. He probably did not display courage and other-regard; he just happened to be in the wrong place at the wrong time. We should most certainly mourn him, but labeling him a "hero" does not do justice to what actually happened, and it does a great injustice to actual heroes, confusing people about the very meaning of the term.

The other thing to remember about role models—and the Stoics understood this very well—is that they are not perfect human beings, for the simple reason that there is no such thing. Moreover, making perfection an integral part of our concept of role model means that we are setting a standard that is impossibly high. Some religions do this of course. For Christians, the model of universally good behavior is Jesus, but that's a tough role model to actually attempt to emulate, since believers are literally trying to be like gods. Bound to fail, we have to accept the divinity's mercy as our path to salvation.

The Stoics, eminently practical and good connoisseurs of human psychology that they were, approached things differently. Seneca wrote an essay on the nature of the wise person, the ideal Stoic role model, or Sage. Here is how he responded to his critics who thought that he was setting the bar too high for anyone to actually succeed at being wise: "You have no cause for saying, as you are wont [sic] to do, that this wise man of ours is nowhere to be found; we do not invent him as an unreal glory of the human race, or conceive a mighty shadow of an untruth, but we have displayed and will display him just as we sketch him, though he may perhaps be uncommon, and only one appears at long intervals; for what is great and transcends the common ordinary type is not often produced; but this very

Marcus Cato himself, the mention of whom started this discussion, was a man who I fancy even surpassed our model."

Marcus Cato, known as Cato the Younger, was a Roman senator and a political opponent of Julius Caesar. Cato was a Roman aristocrat, and as such a product of his time. He was unable to see, for instance, that the Roman Republic he so idolized was highly unequal (though not as much as it would become under the empire he fought to prevent) and founded on slavery and military conquest. For instance, in 72 BCE, he volunteered to fight against the rebel slave Spartacus, clearly not having paused to consider that the revolt might have been a reaction to extreme injustice. Like most Romans, he was probably also not particularly bothered by the clearly inferior position accorded to women in that society. In other words, he would spectacularly fail a modern test as a role model. But that would be exactly the wrong way to look at him, because it would be an attempt to make him a godlike figure capable of doing what no human being can do: completely transcend his own upbringing. Instead, we should assess him by the standards of his own culture and time. By those standards, he was a role model indeed.

Cato was an unusual kid. At fourteen, he asked his tutor Sarpedon why nobody acted to stop the illegal actions of the dictator Lucius Cornelius Sulla, to which Sarpedon replied that people feared Sulla more than they hated him. Cato then said, "Give me a sword, that I might free my country from slavery." Sarpedon never again let Cato play unattended when in Rome, just in case. After he began to study Stoicism, Cato lived very modestly, despite the wealth he inherited. When he was given a military command in Macedon at age twenty-eight, he marched with his men, sharing their food and sleeping quarters. As a result, he was loved by his legionnaires. Later on, in his political career, Cato quickly built a reputation for incorruptibility—a very unusual trait at that, or any, time. As quaestor, he prosecuted Sulla's informers for illegal appropriation of treasury funds and for murder. When he was sent to Cyprus, he managed the public books with absolute integrity (again, a rare thing indeed), raising 7,000 silver talents for the Republic's treasury. To appreciate the enormity of that sum, consider that a Roman talent weighed 32.3 kilograms (71 pounds) and that a single, smaller, Attic talent was sufficient to pay nine man-years of skilled work—or equivalently, a month's wages for a trireme ship's crew of 200.

Eventually, Cato came into open conflict with Julius Caesar, who followed in the steps of Sulla and declared war against the Roman Senate by crossing the river Rubicon with one of his legions, the occasion on which he famously declared, "Alea iacta est" (The die is cast). The rest, as they say, is history: Caesar's forces, after an initial setback, defeated the Senate's army at Pharsalus, in Greece. Cato refused to concede and retreated to Utica, in modern Tunisia. Caesar pursued Cato and his allies and won a final decisive battle at Thapsus. Cato, refusing to be captured alive by his enemy, who would have used him for political gain, did the Roman thing: he attempted to commit suicide with his dagger. Plutarch tells us the rest of the story:

> Cato did not immediately die of the wound; but struggling, fell off the bed, and throwing down a little mathematical table that stood by, made such a noise that the

servants, hearing it, cried out. And immediately his son and all his friends came into the chamber, where, seeing him lie weltering in his own blood, great part of his bowels out of his body, but himself still alive and able to look at them, they all stood in horror. The physician went to him, and would have put in his bowels, which were not pierced, and sewed up the wound; but Cato, recovering himself, and understanding the intention, thrust away the physician, plucked out his own bowels, and tearing open the wound, immediately expired.

Caesar was not pleased, commenting: "Cato, I grudge you your death, as you would have grudged me the preservation of your life." You can appreciate why Seneca thinks of this sort of man as a true Stoic role model.

After all this talk of overcoming the hardships of torture and solitary confinement, or of disemboweling oneself in order not to concede political advantage, you might have the impression that Stoicism is not impossible, but it sure is demanding. As the public philosopher, and my colleague, Nigel Warburton asked me during an interview, "What about ordinary life, where people hardly have to face such extreme situations or display such levels of courage and endurance?"

It's a good question, but the answer is simple enough: it is by hearing about great deeds that we not only become inspired by what human beings at their best can do, but also are implicitly reminded of just how much easier most of our lives actually are. That being the case, it shouldn't really take a lot of courage to stand up to your boss when your coworker is being treated badly, no? I mean, the worst that can happen is that you'll be fired, not put into solitary confinement and tortured. How difficult is it, really, to behave honestly in the course of everyday life, since we are not risking military defeat and the prospect of suicide to save our honor? And yet, imagine how much better the world would be if we all did display just a bit more courage, a slightly more acute sense of justice, more temperance, and more wisdom each day. The Stoic gamble was that hearing about people like Cato, Stockdale, and the others we have encountered here helps us put things into perspective—that is, to become slightly better human beings than we already are.

CHAPTER 10

DISABILITY AND MENTAL ILLNESS

Doing without a wheelchair is not a basic life goal.

—LAWRENCE BECKER, VIDEO ADDRESS TO POST-POLIO
HEALTH INTERNATIONAL

STOICISM IS MEANT TO AID ACTUAL PEOPLE IN LIVING THEIR
lives to the fullest possible extent. But it is another question
whether Stoicism can also be helpful to those who are forced
to live, not simply through challenging circumstances, but
through permanently challenged lives—people who are confined to a wheelchair, for instance, or battling a debilitating
mental illness. The answer appears to be a qualified yes, at
least some of the time. Philosophy is no miracle cure, and it
should not be treated as one.

In this chapter, we will take momentary leave of our
friend Epictetus and meet three modern Stoics who have stories to tell about how their philosophy helped them cope with
the aftermath of polio, with depression, and with autism. We
have seen that the ancients often taught by invoking real and
imaginary role models, from Socrates to the demigod Heracles. The people we will encounter in this chapter are modern

Stoic role models whose thoughts and actions give us much to reflect upon and be inspired by in our own little and big quotidian struggles.

Larry Becker, now a retired professor of philosophy who taught at the College of William and Mary, wrote a fundamental academic book on modern Stoicism. I initially became aware of Larry because of that book, which eventually I spent several months discussing with my friend Greg Lopez and a number of others interested in Stoicism in New York City. Larry's book is not easy to read without some background in philosophy, and the style is, shall we say, unusual. From the beginning, he refers to the Stoics as "us" and "we." Here was someone who evidently took the idea of Stoicism as a personal philosophy very seriously.

It soon turned out that I had no clue as to just *how* seriously! By chance I discovered that my friend and colleague Nick Pappas at the City College of New York, who is an ancient philosophy scholar (meaning a scholar of ancient philosophy, not that he's particularly old), is a good friend and former colleague of Larry's, and so the two of us were introduced.

Larry has been suffering for decades from the aftermath of polio. Nick had told me about heroic feats performed by his friend to overcome the effects of his disability and flourish in his teaching and scholarly career, and this background had of course already put his book and interest in Stoicism into a whole different perspective for me. Then Larry made me aware of a video he had done for Post-Polio Health International, of which he was president and chair from 2006 to 2009. It was watching that video that made me fully appreciate why Larry Becker is a modern role model in the best Stoic tradition.

Larry had polio in his teenage years, back in 1952, prior to the vaccine, and spent a lengthy time in a rehabilitation hospital. Initially he was quadriplegic and confined to an iron lung. After two and a half years of rehabilitation, he had regained the use of his legs, but not of his arms. Larry's breathing was compromised by polio, a condition that has gotten worse with age. Because he cannot use his diaphragm, he breathes with his neck muscles; when he goes to sleep, he stops breathing entirely until his blood CO_2 climbs enough to wake him up. As he wryly put it, "That's inconvenient." So he uses a small portable ventilator for sleeping and for resting during the day. The physical abilities he recovered in the rehabilitation hospital years ago are gradually disappearing as he ages, and it is now impossible for him to teach other than in a one-on-one situation.

In the video, Larry begins by explaining that early on he was able to leave his wheelchair and walk up and down stairs to get to and from his teaching classroom. But things began to get worse in the early 1980s, and he started dreading the idea of going to class or attending faculty meetings (well, all right, everybody dreads faculty meetings). His initial reaction was to say nothing to others and to simply avoid having to walk or climb stairs as much as possible. But he quickly got to the point where he had a hard time dealing with just the four steps he had to negotiate between his office and the open campus. He was spending idle time at his desk, worrying about getting outside, and then about going home in the evening.

His initial analysis was that he was suffering from a phobia, perhaps accompanied by something like panic attacks. So he went to see a psychiatrist who specialized in rehabilitation. The psychiatrist himself was totally blind, which must have made it no cakewalk for him to get through medical school. The psychiatrist's office was in a nice old house, with five uneven steps from the parking lot, four more to the front porch, and no handrails. Not good.

After an initial explanation from Larry, the psychiatrist asked him what was bothering him right at that moment, to which Larry replied, somewhat testily, "I'm bothered by how I'm going to get out of your building." The psychiatrist calmly picked up his phone, called his secretary, and asked her whether they had a ramp running around the back of the building, down to the parking lot. She confirmed that they did. "How do you feel now?" inquired the psychiatrist.

"I feel fine about that," Larry said.

The doctor then went through a series of potential practical solutions to the problem: Can you change office? No. Can the university build you a ramp? Possibly. The doctor told Larry that he had taken subways to get to medical school, and that as a blind man he was terrified of subway platforms. "It's a reasonable fear," he added, "and you'll notice that I chose to practice in a city without subways." At that point Larry began to feel a bit foolish. The university did build a ramp for him, and he got a wheelchair with foot controls. That was a good lesson in practical Stoicism, without the theory.

Larry reflected that these sorts of things had happened to him throughout his life and, moreover, that they happen to everyone, disabled or not. This reflection led him to a number of suggestions to help others develop a personal philosophy about life, whether they live with a disability or not.

Larry's first point is to realize the importance of agency. It has been crucial for him to feel like an agent in the world, not a patient. Some big tasks, however, must be accomplished— for instance, becoming and remaining an agent in the first place. At the beginning of our lives as helpless infants— "entry-level human beings" he calls them—we are "patients," entirely dependent on others. We slowly learn, from scratch, how to be agents. We become adults, taking charge of our lives, claiming and earning our agency (all of which is perfectly compatible with the Stoic doctrine of ethical development, with which we are by now familiar). For Larry, the most devastating disabilities are precisely those that severely limit or entirely erase our agency. Yet he claims that even if polio paralyzes you completely, paralysis itself doesn't permanently rob you of your agency. Nevertheless, you may need to reclaim it, slowly and painfully, as he did. Indeed, he saw the whole question of dealing with his disability as coinciding with his need to reclaim his agency.

After you have reclaimed your agency, Larry points out, you are in the same position as everyone else: you have to become good at *being* an agent. This, he says, requires lining up the following elements: values, preferences, goals, deliberations, decisions, and actions. If these are incoherent, incomplete, or weak, then you are paralyzed no matter what your physical condition happens to be. You can also be paralyzed by indecision, because you are not committed to a particular course of action and wish to keep multiple possibilities open. Facing too many choices on the menu, or too many cars on the dealer's lot, isn't a good thing, as modern cognitive science clearly shows. To complicate things, there is the fact that the world itself changes, requiring constant adjustments to our goals, decisions, and actions. In other words, we need to learn how to maintain agency under changing circumstances. Like airline pilots, we need to keep learning new skills, but unlike airline pilots, we don't have the luxury of learning with simulators. Life only happens once, and we learn "in the air," not in a safe environment. To make things even more stressful, we usually have passengers we care a lot about on board too!

Second, we need to focus on abilities, not disabilities. Larry has learned to disregard his disability, or at least to regard it as a dispreferred indifferent. This requires mastering additional tasks, like keeping the focus incessantly on abilities. The emphasis, for every human being, should be on what we can do, not on what we cannot do. Instead of saying, "I can't do that," say, "I can do it this way."

We also need to practice the Socratic task: know thyself. Knowing our physical and psychological abilities includes knowing our limits. Ignorance, or worse, self-deception about our own abilities can be very dangerous. We need to keep an up-to-date, accurate account of what is possible for us. This will depend not just on our abilities but also on the specific (and variable) physical and social environments in which we find ourselves at different times. Larry also counsels us to train ourselves to recognize when we have lost a good fit between our abilities and our activities. We must develop what he calls an internal alarm system, which will tell us when it's time to stop suffering and begin (or resume) taking charge.

Larry knows from experience that knowing oneself is hard, it takes practice, and it requires some perspective.

Third, we need to develop a life plan. To do this we must take a look at our entire life, make plans, and arrive at decisions "all things considered," as philosophers say. The idea isn't the naive one of figuring out what we want to do in life early on and then just implementing the plan, Soviet-style. Rather, Larry suggests making a habit of reflecting on what is important to us and on the best way to achieve it, and also to continuously revise our life plan, according to our changing abilities and circumstances. Our dynamic plan should be coherent, ambitious, achievable, revisable, and—ideally—compatible with a generally rising level of life satisfaction. In his own case, Larry admits that, by failing to keep things in perspective in the late 1980s, he denied the onset of the late effects of polio; with a better perspective, he would have told himself that maybe his fear of long staircases was not that unreasonable after all.

Fourth, we should strive for internal harmony, which is a matter of constantly attempting to harmonize the components of our (dynamic) life plan. We need to harmonize our spiritual and rational experiences, our desires and our needs, our reason with our actions. "Personally, I think to have a harmonious life is preferable to being an interesting subject for a biographer, a journalist, or a gossiper," Larry wisely observed.

Lastly, Larry cautions us to beware of brick walls. We need to recognize them when we hit them; even better is to see them coming before we hit them hard. The trick here, according to Larry, is to know when to quit: neither a minute too soon nor a minute too late. Avoiding brick walls requires not only that we keep learning about our abilities throughout life, but also that we determine that what looks like a brick wall really is one. "If it is an illusion, then you can go through it; if it is not, then you need to work around it, or go in another direction entirely." The problem, he adds, is that we seem to have trouble figuring out which brick walls are worth worrying about and which ones we should try to tear down. The way Larry deals with this problem is by going back to the basics. First he identifies his fundamental life goals and commitments: to his wife of forty-six years and to the goals of their life together; to his professional objectives; and to the creation of a truly physically and socially hospitable environment for everyone. Only when these commitments are at stake is he willing to stop if he encounters an actual brick wall, and only if he hits it pretty hard. Ramps, in Larry's estimation, don't qualify: "Doing without a wheelchair is not a basic life goal."

It is hard for me to add something meaningful here. I am truly in awe of a decent human being who is a serious scholar, a committed Stoic, and someone who has clearly lived his philosophy under very challenging circumstances. I'll try to remember Larry the next time I think I've hit a brick wall that much more likely is just an illusion conjured by my self-centered imagination. As Epictetus famously put it: "Bear and forbear."

Our second example of a modern Stoic who has used his philosophy to manage a difficult situation is Andrew Overby and his fight against depression. Unlike the case of Larry,

I have not met Andrew, at least not yet. Our acquaintance, which I'm not positive is reciprocal, is through blogs and social networks. Of course the reader should keep in mind that in all these cases I am definitely not speaking from personal experience: Fate has, so far, been kind enough to not involve me in anything as serious as what we are talking about. Nonetheless, the great thing about human beings is that we can communicate our thoughts and emotions to others, not just in person but through the power of the written word. Although we will never know exactly what it is like to be another person, we can certainly gain enough understanding to empathize.

Andrew describes what, from his vantage point, Stoicism can do under his circumstances. Again, this description isn't coming from someone like me, who has never experienced depression and could only give theoretical advice to others who find themselves in truly difficult circumstances. Rather, Andrew's case illustrates practical philosophy at its best—through the testimony of a human being who discovered firsthand what is and is not helpful to him in solving his problem. Just as we have seen with Larry, Andrew most certainly does not claim that Stoicism can somehow magically cure depression. Nevertheless, he did find something helpful in the practice of Stoicism.

To begin with, he says that one of the crucial things for people affected by depression is to constantly monitor themselves and their mental condition. If there is anything that Stoicism trains people to do it is to monitor their own reactions and reflect critically on how they perceive and interpret the world.

When Andrew wrote about his encounter with Stoicism, he was a young man of twenty-four suffering from a depression that stemmed in part from the gulf he had gradually realized existed between his expectations about his life and the world, on the one hand, and his life and the world as they were, on the other hand. It seemed like reassessment and perhaps an attempt at partial detachment were in order. Andrew began to read about Stoicism because he had heard that it is similar in many ways to Buddhism, and also because during a visit to the Clinton Library in Arkansas he had discovered that President Clinton held Marcus Aurelius, the Stoic emperor-philosopher, in high regard. (I will leave to others a discussion of whether Bill Clinton behaved anything like a Stoic during his life and career.) Andrew was intrigued. Moreover, one goal of Stoic philosophy, especially in its Roman period, was to achieve tranquillity—something that is good for any human being, but especially for someone suffering from depression. The Stoics attempted to do so by cultivating positive emotions and monitoring and rejecting negative ones. (We will take a closer look at these techniques in due time.) Andrew was also attracted by the Stoic spirit of communality with the rest of humanity, its rejection of attachment to the sort of external goods that characterize our hyper-consumerist society, and its emphasis on duty toward others and equanimity in the face of adversity.

Through Stoicism, Andrew learned to turn depression into an asset of sorts. As he explains: "Depressed people are rather self-aware; in fact, they are too self-aware, and too negatively so, often deriding themselves for small infractions of their own idealized standards, putting themselves down for not being perfect even in a world they recognize as being full of imperfections and human capital squandered. Part of depression is fixating on failures in the past, ruminating continually on past events or circumstances, and even drawing a kind of negative confidence from them. This type of thinking is antithetical to good outcomes at the present time, at least the vast majority of the time. It causes failure in the present, building a feedback loop whose hunger cannot be easily filled. One failure builds atop another, and now another."

Once Andrew realized this connection between negative thinking and depression, his mind turned immediately to Epictetus's dichotomy of control. Things under our control include our decisions and behaviors; things not under our control include the circumstances we find ourselves in, as well as other people's thoughts and actions. Of course, it's not like someone is depressed, reads lines in the *Discourses* or the *Handbook* that seem to speak to his situation, and then voilà!—everything is hunky-dory. But Andrew kept reading and reflecting. Indeed, the Stoics taught that it is with mindful repetition that we change our own behaviors and even our internal feelings—something confirmed by a number of modern psychotherapies that are effective for the treatment of depression and other conditions.

Another aspect of Stoicism that Andrew found particularly helpful was the philosophy's emphasis on using adversity as a training ground for life. Marcus Aurelius perhaps expressed the idea most forcefully, in the very same *Meditations* so admired by Bill Clinton: "The art of life is more like the wrestler's art than the dancer's, in respect of this, that it should stand ready and firm to meet onsets that are sudden and unexpected." In a sort of life judo, the Stoic faces up to adversity by treating life itself as a wrestler in the training ring, as an opponent who is not (necessarily) out to beat us, but whose purpose is to keep us on our toes; the Stoic becomes eager to face his opponent because that's the way toward self-improvement. As the modern Stoic Bill Irvine puts it: "One of the most interesting developments in my practice of Stoicism has been my transformation from someone who dreaded insults into an insult connoisseur. For one thing, I have become a collector of insults: On being insulted, I analyze and categorize the insult. For another thing, I look forward to being insulted inasmuch as it affords me the opportunity to perfect my 'insult game.' I know this sounds strange, but one consequence of the practice of Stoicism is that one seeks opportunities to put Stoic techniques to work." Strange, yes, but I can attest to the same liberating and empowering feeling, and so can Andrew.

His testimony emphasizes two other aspects of Stoic practice that are particularly helpful to a depressed person, one of them in a somewhat counterintuitive fashion. The first is Epictetus's insistence that we look at "impressions," that is, at our first reactions to what the world presents us with, and realize that in many cases they are not what they seem. Think of Irvine's "insult game": what someone says to us is his opinion, which may or may not be grounded in fact. Whether we perceive someone else's remark as an insult or not is entirely up to us, quite regardless of the intention of our interlocutor. Someone may call me fat, as indeed happened somewhat frequently when I was a young boy. Well, is it true? At one time in my life it was. In which case, why get offended? What does it even mean to feel insulted by a fact? Conversely, is it not true? Then the fellow who hurled the insult is both childish in his behavior and factually wrong. How is that going to injure *me*? If anything, he is the one who loses in the confrontation. Here is how our Epictetus put it to me, as a friendly challenge: "Stand by a stone and slander it: what effect will you produce? If a man then listens like a stone, what advantage has the slanderer? . . . 'I have done you an outrage.' May it turn out to your good."

The second aspect of Stoic practice that—perhaps surprisingly—Andrew found very helpful was what modern Stoics call negative visualization. The basic idea, again adopted by modern cognitive behavioral therapy and similar approaches, is to regularly focus on potentially bad scenarios, repeating to yourself that they are not in fact as bad as they may seem, because you have the inner resources to deal with them. The negative visualization exercise, what the ancient Romans called *premeditatio malorum* (literally, foreseeing bad stuff), may focus on something as mundane as the irritation you feel when someone cuts you off in traffic or on events as critical as the death of a loved one, or even your own.

Now, why would anyone, let alone someone who is depressed, want to imagine the worst on purpose? Well, for one thing there is the empirical observation that it actually works: visualizing negative happenings decreases our fear of them and mentally prepares us to deal with the crisis when and if it ensues. But there is a flip side to visualizing the negative: we gain a renewed sense of gratitude and appreciation for all the times when bad things do *not* happen to us, when we leisurely drive down the road on a beautiful day or enjoy the presence of our loved ones because they are very much alive and well.

I don't even know the name of my third fellow Stoic, as the essay I read by her or him was published anonymously. And I certainly cannot relate to what she (I will assume she's a woman for the sake of simplicity) is going through, having been diagnosed with autism spectrum disorder ten years before writing her article. That was accompanied by depression at the realization that her dream of an academic career was not to be—not because of external obstacles to becoming and finding a job as a historian, as formidable as those can be, but because of her inner obstacles: she simply couldn't cope with the social environment of the modern academy. Indeed, her life was dominated by fear of failure and lack of self-confidence, which eventually landed her in a psychiatric hospital. When she was released, she rediscovered Stoicism. She had read about it as a youngster, in a popular book of philosophy for teens, Jostein Gaarder's *Sophie's World.* Now she Googled "cognitive behavioral therapy," seeking practical help, and found the website of a practitioner who traced the roots of the approach to Buddhism and Stoicism.

She began to read, and eventually she discovered that the Stoic to whom she responded the most was the Roman playwright and orator Seneca. (I have observed this fascinating, if anecdotal, thing about modern Stoics: depending, presumably, on personality, we tend to have a favorite ancient and to be drawn to his particular way of interpreting the philosophy. My favorite Stoic, obviously, is Epictetus.) Seneca wrote about self-knowledge and suggested that sometimes we are the worst obstacles to our own improvement: we see where we should go, which is where we want to go, and yet somehow we can't pick ourselves up and begin the journey. This observation obviously resonated with our anonymous author: "The problem with some people in the spectrum is knowing what is good for oneself. Some people with autism reportedly struggle with finding a sense of purpose for most of their lives."

A second aspect of Stoic philosophy that spoke to our autistic author was Seneca's insistence on the social dimension of human existence. In a famous passage, he says: "Our relations with one another are like a stone arch, which would collapse if the stones did not mutually support each other, and which is upheld in this very way." Relating to others in a socially useful fashion is still the author's biggest challenge, but at least she now has her goals much more clearly in mind, goals that are being guided by her understanding of Stoicism. And as Seneca keeps telling her every time she turns to him: "I do not know whether I shall make progress; but I should prefer to lack success rather than to lack faith."

The three cases we have briefly examined here have something fundamental in common: for Larry, just as for Andrew and the anonymous writer, Stoicism triggered a change in perspective, a profound alteration in how they looked at their lives. Importantly, this is precisely what the philosophy is *meant* to do: all the major Stoic authors insist that it is crucial that we reflect on our condition and truly make an effort to see things in a different light, one that is both more rational and more compassionate. And no, those two requirements are most definitely not at odds with each other, certainly not from a Stoic point of view. Such a change in perspective helps people to cope better with their situation. Stoicism is predictably often accused of promoting passive acceptance of things—despite the fact that the Stoics we know of were most definitely men and women of action, bent on changing the world for the better to the extent that it was in their power to do so. Regardless, coping is an essential human skill that is obviously helpful not just to people confined to wheelchairs, those battling depression, or those affected by autism. Coping skills are useful to all of us, since we will always encounter tough situations in life with which we must come to terms.

Finally, the combination of seeing, and therefore understanding, things differently and the empowerment that derives from the ability to cope sometimes opens up new ways of dealing with our problems that perhaps we had not thought of before—as when the psychiatrist pointed out to Larry (who felt a bit foolish) a couple of obvious solutions to his problem, one of which turned out to be eminently practical. Stoicism is no silver bullet. But any philosophy that can do these things, even under the very challenging conditions we have encountered in this chapter, certainly deserves our attention and perhaps a shot at being practiced.

PART III

THE DISCIPLINE OF ASSENT:
HOW TO REACT TO SITUATIONS

CHAPTER 11

ON DEATH AND SUICIDE

I must die, must I? If at once, then I am dying: if soon, I dine now, as it is time for dinner, and afterwards when the time comes I will die.

—EPICTETUS, *DISCOURSES*, I.1

THE ANCIENT STOICS WERE VERY CONCERNED WITH DEATH. Actually, "concerned" is precisely the wrong word. They were aware of death and of the importance that human beings attach to it, but they developed a very unusual and empowering view of it.

I must confess that I've had long and hard conversations with Epictetus about this topic: the thought of death used to bother me deeply. Indeed, there was a time in my life when I was thinking about it almost every day, and on some days more than once. I don't want you to get the impression that I was ever the brooding type, prone to depressive thoughts. On the contrary, I've always been reasonably optimistic about life, enjoying or doing my best with whatever Fortune sends my way (and she has sent a lot, thankfully). Moreover, I am a biologist. I know that death is a natural occurrence, the result of the particular evolutionary pathway taken by our ancestors eons ago. (If we were bacteria, for instance, we wouldn't die of old age, only of accidents; then again, we wouldn't be able to develop philosophies of life either.) Still, the thought of my consciousness one day ceasing to exist did upset me. Things started to change when I first read Epictetus's statement at the beginning of this chapter. I laughed out loud and thought, *What an unbelievably lighthearted attitude toward what most people think is the most dreadful thing of all.*

Epictetus also explained to me why I was so bothered: "Why does an as of wheat grow? Is it not that it may ripen in the sun? And if it is ripened is it not that it may be reaped, for it is not a thing apart? If it had feelings then, ought it to pray never to be reaped at any time? But this is a curse upon wheat—to pray that it should never be reaped. In like manner know that you are cursing men when you pray for them not to die: it is like a prayer not to be ripened, not to be reaped. But we men, being creatures whose fate it is to be reaped, are also made aware of this very fact, that we are destined for reaping, and so we are angry; for we do not know who we are, nor have we studied human things as those who are skilled in horses study the concerns of horses."

This is an intriguing passage. Epictetus sets forth three interlinked ideas. To begin with, we are no different from other living beings: like the wheat whose as are destined to ripen in the sun, we too are destined for "reaping." The Stoics took destiny more literally than many of us do today, since they believed in some sort of cosmic Providence. But even from a thoroughly modern scientific point of view, we can see that we are one of millions of living species on one of what are probably billions of habitable planets in the universe.

The second point Epictetus makes is crucial: we are so distraught about the prospect of our own death precisely because, unlike wheat and most other species on earth presumably, we are capable of contemplating that thought. And yet, knowing something does not change the nature of the thing of course—it just changes our attitude about it. This line of thought thus leads straight back to the fundamental Stoic idea of the dichotomy of control: death itself is not under our control (it will happen one way or another), but how we think about death most definitely is under our control. That's the part we can and need to work on.

This second point leads to the third one: the analogy between studying human affairs and—of all things—studying horses. Epictetus is reminding us that if we are afraid of death, then it is out of ignorance: if we knew or truly understood more about the human condition—as a horse trainer knows and understands horses—then we wouldn't react the way we do to the prospect of our own death.

All of the above notwithstanding, Epictetus sensed that I wasn't quite convinced, so he changed tactics, as any good teacher does when faced with a promising student who nevertheless just refuses to see an important point: "Will you realize once for all that it is not death that is the source of all man's evils, and of a mean and cowardly spirit, but rather the fear of death? Against this fear then I would have you discipline yourself; to this let all your reasonings, your lectures, and your trainings be directed; and then you will know that only so do men achieve their freedom." This is an idea also taken up by other Stoics, like Seneca, and by later figures influenced by Stoicism, such as Montaigne: if there is one thing that philosophy ought to be good for, it is to make us better understand the human condition by showing us not only how to live to our best but to accept the fact that death is nothing to be afraid of. Even the Stoics' archrivals, the Epicureans, thoroughly agreed. As the founder of their school wrote in his "Letter to Menoeceus": "Death, therefore, the most awful of evils, is nothing to us, seeing that, when we are, death is not come, and, when death is come, we are not."

What, then, if I fall ill? I asked Epictetus, thinking that perhaps it isn't death but the process of dying that is the real issue. "You shall bear illness well." Of course, but who shall tend me? "God, and your friends." But I shall lie on a hard bed. "But you can do it like a man." I shall not have a proper house. "If you have one, you will be ill all the same." Tough teacher, isn't he? But by now all of this makes perfect sense from within the Stoic framework, right? It is a fact of life that we are stricken by illnesses, and for most of us one of them will eventually kill us. And we ought to consider ourselves lucky if we do have friends or loved ones nearby—it will mean that we have been decent-enough people to maintain such ties with the rest of humanity. Those around us cannot cure our illness or save us from death, but they can accompany us part of the way, comforting us before we get there. And of course it would be better to end our journey in a proper house and on a soft bed, but, really, compared to what will be happening and should be absorbing our full attention, those are minor details.

So, inevitably, the time will come to die, I continued. "What do you mean by 'die'?" Epictetus corrected me. "Do not use fine words, but state the facts as they are. Now is the time for your material part to be restored to the elements of which it was composed. What is there dreadful in that? What loss to the universe will this mean, what strange or irrational event?" Again, the reassuring voice of calm reason. Again, the invitation to take a broader perspective on things rather than be focused on one's own self. The astronomer Carl Sagan, one of my scientific role models when I was a kid, invited us to reflect on the fact that we literally are stardust: the chemical elements of which we are made originated after the explosion of a supernova somewhere in the neighborhood of the solar system, and billions of years of evolution later such matter became the very molecules that constitute our bodies. It is a wonderful, awe-inspiring thought. But the converse of that is what Epictetus is getting at: we will, again literally, return to dust, recycling our chemicals, allowing new living beings to take our place in the workings of the universe. It doesn't matter whether those workings have a point or whether they are just what they are: either way, we came from cosmic dust and we will return to cosmic dust. If anything, this should make us even more appreciative of the infinitesimal interval, from a cosmic perspective, during which we are alive and we eat, drink, and love. Regret at the anticipation that this interval will end is not just irrational but entirely unhelpful.

And yet, some people are not persuaded of this at all. On the contrary, a number of techno-optimists think that death is a disease that should be cured, and they are investing good money in the effort. Broadly speaking, they call themselves

"Transhumanists," and quite a few of them can be found among the white male millionaires in Silicon Valley, where many of the world's most influential tech companies are located. Perhaps the most famous and influential of the bunch is Ray Kurzweil, a futurist (someone who thinks he can study and predict the future) currently working at Google to develop a software capable of understanding natural language.

Kurzweil has a number of important achievements under his belt, including the development of the first omni-font optical character recognition system. Age sixty-eight at the time of this writing, he has been arguing for some time that the way to immortality will be to upload our consciousness into a computer, which he claims will be possible any day now. Indeed, we better manage that feat before the so-called Singularity, a term invented by the mathematician Stanisław Ulam to describe the moment when computers will outsmart people and begin to drive technological progress independently—and perhaps even in spite—of humanity itself.

This is not the place to explain why I think the whole idea of a Singularity is predicated on a fundamental misunderstanding of the nature of intelligence, or why "uploading" our consciousness to a computer is extremely unlikely to ever be possible, since consciousness is neither a thing nor a piece of software. Here I'm more interested in the chutzpah displayed by people like Kurzweil as well as by his almost cultlike following, who think of themselves as so important that they ought to, godlike, transcend the laws of nature itself, never mind the fact that they are spending inordinate amounts of money and energy that could be directed toward ameliorating

actual, urgent problems the world faces right now, or the disastrous ethical and environmental consequences of their success
(if it were possible). Who, exactly, would have access to the
new technology, and at what price? If we succeed in becoming physically immortal—the alternative to uploading hoped
for by some Transhumanists—will we keep having children?
If so, how would an already diseased planet sustain the thirst
for natural resources of a population that grows so relentlessly
and manage its ever-escalating production of waste products?
Ah, but we will expand beyond Earth! We shall colonize other
worlds! Never mind that we still don't know of any other habitable worlds in the galaxy, or that we have no clue about how to
get to them, if they're out there. The more I think about Trans-
humanism the more the word *hubris,* famously invented by the
Greeks precisely for such thinking, seems awfully appropriate.

The likes of Kurzweil simply don't want to leave the party,
it seems to me, no matter what the cost, and regardless of
how privileged they have been while attending it. Which is
why I imagine him having this conversation with Epictetus:
"No, I wanted to go on feasting." "Yes, those at the Mysteries
too want to go on with the ceremony, and those at Olympia
to see fresh competitors, but the festival is at an end. Leave it
and depart, in a thankful and modest spirit; make room for
others. Others must come into being, even as you did, and
being born must have room and dwellings and necessaries.
But if the first comers do not retire, what is left for them?
Why will nothing satisfy or content you? Why do you crowd
the world's room?" Which brings me to the second, far more
delicate, topic of this chapter, and one to which the Stoics

devoted a lot of thought that I think is very much of relevance to us moderns: suicide.

On the weekend of July 23 and 24, 2016, the performance artist Betsy Davis hosted a party with thirty or so of her closest friends and family. The occasion was joyous, with people playing cello and harmonica, drinking cocktails and eating pizza, and watching one of Betsy's favorite movies, *The Dance of Reality*. A bit before sunset on Sunday the guests left, and Betsy watched the sunset on her wraparound porch. Shortly after, in the presence of her caretaker, her doctor, her massage therapist, and her sister, Betsy took a cocktail of morphine, pentobarbital, and chloral hydrate prescribed by her doctor and died peacefully.

You see, Betsy was suffering from amyotrophic lateral sclerosis, or ALS, also known as Lou Gehrig's disease. She had almost completely lost control of her muscles; at forty-one, she not only was unable to perform but could no longer brush her teeth or scratch an itch, let alone stand. Her speech was slurred and had to be translated to others. She took the dignified way out, thanks to the recently enacted California law on assisted suicide. Hers was a beautiful, heart-wrenching story, which I related to Epictetus. "If it is not to your profit, the door stands open: if it is to your profit, bear it. For in every event the door must stand open and then we have no trouble," he calmly replied. The "open door" was the standard phrase he used with his students whenever he wanted to talk about suicide. Seeing my puzzlement, he elaborated: "Suppose someone made the room smoke. If the smoke is moderate I will stay: if excessive,

I go out: for one must remember and hold fast to this, that the door is open. The order comes, 'Do not dwell in Nicopolis.' I will not. 'Nor in Athens.' I give up Athens. 'Nor in Rome.' I give up Rome. 'Dwell in Gyara.' I dwell in Gyara: but this seems to me a very smoky room indeed, and I depart where no one shall hinder me from dwelling: for that dwelling is open to every man."

Before we examine this more closely, allow me to insert an interesting historical parenthesis about Gyara, apparently the place where Epictetus thought one might have a hard enough time standing to actually consider walking through "the open door." Gyara is a small Greek island in the Cyclades to which the ancient Romans exiled troublemakers. One such troublemaker was none other than Musonius Rufus, Epictetus's teacher, who was sent there by the emperor Nero for allegedly participating in the Pisonian conspiracy—a charge unlikely to have been true. (That was the second time Musonius was sent into exile.) The practice of sending exiles to the island, which is apparently pretty arid, was later resurrected by the military junta that controlled Greece from 1967 to 1974. This time it was leftist intellectuals who played the part of the Stoics; about 22,000 of them were sent there. However bad the conditions are on Gyara, it must be said that Musonius may have been tougher than even Epictetus, since he didn't choose the open door, but rather waited on the island until he was recalled to Rome.

Getting back to Epictetus, there are a number of important things to notice in the passage just quoted. To begin with, he very clearly states that deciding whether or not to walk through the "door" is a matter of personal judgment, pertinent to specific situations. *If* the situation is truly unbearable *for you*, then you have the option to leave. Second, and crucially, the door must stand open and then we will have no trouble: what will make it possible for us to withstand harsh conditions and very difficult periods in our lives will be precisely that we always have an alternative course of action at our disposal. Just as, for the Stoics, death itself is what gives urgent meaning to life, the possibility of leaving life voluntarily gives us the courage to do what is right under otherwise unbearable circumstances. Finally, notice the reference to the coming of an "order" to leave. Scholars of Epictetus have shown that he is talking about God here, but in a very subtle way, which is once again compatible with either a religious or a secular reading.

Recall that Epictetus, more so than other Stoics, believed in Providence, that is, in a general plan for the cosmos. That plan, however, was not laid out by a personal God who answers prayers or is concerned with the fate of individuals. Epictetus explained the idea to me using yet another analogy: "For the foot (for instance), I shall say it is natural to be clean, but if you take it as a foot and not as a detached thing, it will be fitting for it to walk in the mud and tread upon thorns and sometimes to be cut off for the sake of the whole body: or else it will cease to be a foot. We must hold exactly the same sort of view about ourselves." That explains the sense in which someone might receive a "call" to cut himself off the rest of the (cosmic) body, so to speak. But how are we to know about the call? How do we interpret the will of the universe? We make use of reason. It is therefore entirely up to us, individually, to examine the situation and decide whether we hear the call of the cosmos—so to speak—or not. It is, in other words, our own judgment that tells us whether it is time to walk through the open door or whether we should stay and fight another day.

Being practical philosophers, the Stoics fine-tuned their ability to make such judgments by reflecting on examples from the past, just as the story of Betsy Davis had me reflecting on disease and mortality. The very first mention of a Stoic committing suicide concerns Zeno of Cyprus, the founder of Stoicism. Diogenes Laertius, in his *Lives of the Eminent Philosophers*, tells a number of different stories about how Zeno died (only one of which can be true, obviously). One says that, being old, frail, and in pain, he decided that he had nothing more to contribute to society, so he starved himself to death. This may or may not have happened, but the story is significant because it introduces the idea that it is acceptable for Stoics to walk through the open door under certain circumstances, given that it is possible that the very founder of the school did it.

There are several more examples from Stoic lore, but I'll mention just two of them in order to broaden our view of the topic. We have already encountered Cato the Younger, who literally tore his guts out so as not to fall into the hands of Julius Caesar. The last example is Seneca, a rather controversial figure even within Stoic circles. It is not at all clear just how much Seneca lived up to his own philosophy, given his involvement with Nero's regime. He has been portrayed as everything from a hypocritical schemer to a secular saint, with the truth likely being somewhere in the middle: he was a flawed man (as he himself repeatedly wrote) who tried his best under nearly impossible circumstances. Seneca succeeded in guiding Nero and containing the damage for the first five years of his reign, even if he eventually lost control of the increasingly unhinged emperor. Regardless, as mentioned earlier, he was suspected of being part of the Pisonian conspiracy that sent Musonius into exile, also probably on trumped-up charges. Nero ordered Seneca to commit suicide, which he did, at age sixty-nine. He could have resisted (probably in vain), tried to escape, or pleaded for his life, as many others did. Instead, he chose a dignified exit, in part to retain his integrity, and in part to preserve at least some of the family assets so that surviving relatives could inherit them.

I've brought up the examples of Zeno, Cato, and Seneca, with all the due historical caveats, because they illustrate five different reasons for walking through the open door. Zeno did so because he was in increasingly unbearable pain, and he also felt that he had become useless to society—not very different from the case of Betsy Davis. Cato walked through the open door for principled reasons in defense of a political cause. Seneca did so as a matter of personal dignity and to safeguard the people he was leaving behind. (To this list one can add the attempted suicide of James Stockdale.) Some of these reasons for committing suicide are being debated today in military, moral, and medical circles, so that the Stoics still have very much to contribute to our evolving view of the world. We certainly regard as heroes those people who sacrifice their lives for the greater good, and an increasing number of countries are allowing, or at least considering, forms of assisted suicide like the one made possible by California lawmakers to aid people who feel, as seemed to be the case with Zeno twenty-three centuries ago, that they are at the end of their life. Of course, these notions are controversial, as political suicide can be as virtuous as Cato's (or Stockdale's, had he succeeded), but also as horrible as that of modern-day suicide bombers. And ending our lives on our own terms is seen as empowering by some but as a sacrilege against the sanctity of life by others.

Then there is the danger that someone may commit suicide for no good reason. A Stoic rationale should never be deployed, for instance, in the case of people who are mentally ill and require aid in recovering, not in ending, their life. Similarly, there are trivial excuses to commit suicide that would most certainly not receive the approval of a Stoic. For instance, after the publication of Goethe's *The Sorrows of Young Werther* in 1774, there were a number of copycat suicides among young men who fancied themselves to be real-life versions of the story's protagonist. This led to the banning of the book in several places. In 1974 the sociologist David Phillips coined the term "Werther effect" to refer to the general phenomenon of so-called suicide contagion, often inspired by the suicide of celebrities, fictional or otherwise.

Epictetus, ever the wise man, was aware of this danger, and made it clear to me that a light attitude toward taking one's own life was not the Stoic way: "Let me describe another state of mind to be found in those who hear these precepts amiss. A friend of mine, for instance, determined for no reason to starve himself. I learnt of it when he was in the third day of his fasting, and went and asked him what had happened. 'I have decided,' said he. Yes, but, for all that, say what it was that persuaded you; for if your decision was right, here we are at your side ready to help you to leave this life, but, if your decision was against reason, then change your mind. 'A man must abide by his decisions.' What are you doing, man? Not all decisions, but right decisions." Epictetus added: "Stay where you are, and depart not without reason."

CHAPTER 12

HOW TO DEAL WITH ANGER, ANXIETY, AND LONELINESS

> Wherever I go, there is the sun, there is the moon, there are the stars, dreams, auguries, conversation with the gods.
>
> —EPICTETUS, *DISCOURSES*, III.22

PHILOSOPHERS ARE OFTEN CARICATURED AS ALOOF, FOREVER engaged in navel-gazing of no interest to the rest of us. Or worse: they may simply be intellectual frauds, pretending to think deep thoughts while in fact they are peddling either nonsense or trivialities disguised by incomprehensible language. Already in 423 BCE, the great Greek playwright Aristophanes made fun of Socrates in *The Clouds*, depicting him as a sophist (not a compliment, neither then nor ever since), though apparently the then-forty-five-year-old sage took it in stride: it is reported that when some foreigners who were attending the play asked, "Who is this Socrates?" he cheerfully stood up in order to be identified by the crowd in the theater.

Perhaps in reaction to this intellectual excess, real or perceived as it may have been, the Hellenistic (immediately post-Socratic) philosophies all tended to emphasize pragmatism—and none more so, arguably, than Stoicism. Little is more pragmatic than learning to manage anger, anxiety, and loneliness, three major plagues of modern life. Of course, once again, this isn't your standard self-help book promising silver bullets: we are going to deal with these issues calmly, reasonably, and with realistic expectations, just as a proper Stoic would do.

This is an attitude that, of course, I learned from our friend during one of our conversations, when he told me:

> Yesterday I had an iron lamp beside my household gods, and hearing a noise I rushed to the window. I found the lamp had been carried off. I reasoned with myself, that the man who took it yielded to some plausible feeling. What do I conclude? Tomorrow, I say, you will find one of earthenware. I lost my lamp, because in the matter of vigilance the thief was a stronger man than I. But he bought his lamp for this price: for a lamp he became a thief, for a lamp he broke his faith, for a lamp he became a brute.

As usual, there is a lot packed into what Epictetus is saying, and it took some mulling over his words before I fully appreciated his take. First off, notice that he is not distraught or angry, but matter-of-fact; moreover, he immediately reaches a couple of pragmatic conclusions: that what he lost was easily replaceable (tomorrow I will find another lamp), and that if he wishes to avoid another theft, perhaps he should opt for a cheaper but equally effective item (a lamp of earthenware, rather than iron), because it just isn't worthwhile trying to beat a thief at the vigilance game. Then comes the analysis of the deeper meaning of the incident: Epictetus acknowledges that the thief must have yielded to some plausible feeling—he must have reckoned that what he was doing was worth the price. But our sage disagrees with the judgment of the thief, whose conclusion he finds highly questionable: he gained an iron lamp, but in the transaction he lost something much more precious—his integrity.

I had an unfortunate opportunity to test Epictetus's teachings while I was writing this book. I had just boarded the A-line subway train in Rome with my companion; we were on our way to meet my brother and his wife for a leisurely evening. While entering the train car, I felt an unusually strong resistance from a guy nearby, who was forcefully pushing back despite the fact that there was ample room for both of us in the car, which was crowded but not unbearably so. When I finally realized—a few seconds later—what was actually going on, it was too late: while I was being distracted by the unyielding fellow, his friend lifted my wallet from the left front pocket of my trousers and swiftly exited the subway car just before the doors closed. The thief had indeed beaten me at the vigilance game, and kudos to him for his dexterity. My first impression, as the Stoics would say, was one of surprise and frustration at having been fooled. But my mind again quickly went back to Epictetus, and I steadfastly refused to grant assent to that impression. Okay, I had lost my wallet, some cash, and a few credit cards that needed to be blocked. Oh, and my driver's license, which had to be replaced. With good modern electronic technologies, taking care of all that took only a few keystrokes on my smart phone (which was still in my other front pocket!) and a few days' wait. But the thief had lost his integrity in the bargain. Before my practice of Stoicism, an experience like this would probably have made me angry and resentful for the rest of the evening, which would not have done any of us any good (nor would that response have affected the thief or brought back my wallet). Instead, it took only a few minutes to mentally process what had taken place, and by the time we met my brother and his wife all was good with my mind, which had returned to a more tranquil state, and we were able to enjoy a nice evening at the movies.

Neither Epictetus's story about the lamp nor my subway incident should be interpreted as counseling a fatalistic or defeatist attitude. Rather, both suggest that we step back and analyze a situation more rationally, always keeping in mind the dichotomy of control between what is and is not in our power. It is not in our power to make thievery disappear from the world, but it is in our power to engage in a battle of attention with thieves, if we think that's worth our efforts and time. It is not in our power to change the robber's judgment that forgoing his integrity in exchange for a lamp or a wallet is a good bargain, but it is in our power to make the reverse judgment ourselves.

Rephrasings, you may have noticed, are important in Stoicism. There are correspondences in Christianity (hate the sin, not the sinner), and according to modern psychological research, recasting a situation is a crucial component of anger and emotional management. Still, I was wondering whether Epictetus wasn't a bit too casual about his attitude toward robbery and crime, so I pointed that out to him. I should have seen the response coming: "'What!' you say. 'Ought not this robber and this adulterer to be put to death?' Nay, say not so, but rather, 'Should I not destroy this man who is in error and delusion about the greatest matters and is blinded not merely in the vision which distinguishes white and black, but in the judgement which distinguishes good and evil?' If you put it this way, you will recognize how inhuman your words are; that it is like saying, 'Should I not kill this blind man, or this deaf one?'" I actually hadn't suggested anything like the death penalty, but the point was well taken: if we understand the ancient Greek concept of *amathia*, we know that it is more helpful to think of people who do bad things as mistaken and therefore to be pitied and helped if possible, not condemned as evil. Although not very much practiced, especially in the United States, this same idea is behind some of the most progressive, and effective, approaches to reforming criminals as implemented, for instance, in a number of European countries.

It is rather instructive to look at the advice of the American Psychological Association for people dealing with anger and frustration, because it very closely resembles the early intuitions of the Stoics—strengthened, of course, by a significant amount of systematic empirical findings. To begin with, the APA counsels engaging in a series of relaxation techniques. These include deep breathing (from the diaphragm, not the chest), coupled with a simple and meaningful mantra. You can also use imagery—visualizing, for instance, a calming or pleasant situation—and engage in some sort of nonstrenuous exercise, like yoga stretching. Although the Stoics didn't deploy the concept of mantra, they constantly advised practitioners to keep simple, pithy phrases at hand and to reach for them as soon as they saw trouble. Indeed, the entire *Enchiridion*, Arrian's summary of Epictetus's *Discourses*, can be considered a handy set of quick reminders of crucial points for use on the spur of the moment. And Seneca explicitly advised taking a deep breath and going for a walk around the block upon first feeling the uncontrollable rise of rage, which he considered a type of temporary madness. He also said, in his letters to his friend Lucilius, that it is good to exercise regularly, even in old age, not just because exercise keeps the body in decent shape, but because it has a calming effect on the mind. I have found all of this advice to be very effective: my favorite immediate reaction, whenever I sense that I'm beginning to lose control, is to excuse myself, retreat to a quiet place where I can do a little deep breathing (even a bathroom will do!), and mentally repeat my favorite mantra: bear and forbear, which is a standard Epictetian phrase.

This advice, a sort of physiological and mental first-aid kit, is useful for immediate crises, but a number of longer-term strategies must also be deployed if anger is to be effectively managed, according to the APA. One set of strategies involves cognitive restructuring, of which we have seen plenty of Stoic examples, including the ones just discussed. The APA tells us to change standard phrases like "this is terrible!" to something along the lines of "I'd rather not have to deal with this, but I can manage it, and getting angry isn't going to help me at all." Moreover, the suggestion is to transform demands into desires, in recognition that the world isn't just going to bow down to whatever we like. This is very similar to the modern Stoic idea, proposed by Bill Irvine, of learning to internalize goals: I desire (not want or need) a promotion, so I'm going to do my best to deserve it. Whether I actually get it or not is not under my control, because it depends on a number of factors external to my will. As an APA article on anger management—which could easily have been written by Epictetus—reminds us: "Logic defeats anger, because anger, even when it's justified, can quickly become irrational. So use cold hard logic on yourself."

Next, the APA advises us to engage in problem-solving (rather than complaining), but warns us against a common fallacy: we need to realize that—contra common cultural belief—it just isn't the case that every problem has a solution. We therefore need to cut ourselves some slack for not being able to solve everything, so long as we have done all we can reasonably do under the circumstances. Don't focus on just finding a solution, the APA advises, but on how to handle the entire situation, including the possibility of not succeeding in the endeavor. Again, echoes of ancient wisdom abound here.

Another crucial way of handling anger is classified by the APA as "better communication," specifically better communication with people who make you angry. Interestingly, a large component of this advice relies again on Stoic precepts: we should try to describe the situation making us angry as dispassionately and accurately as possible, what Epictetus called giving assent to (or withdrawing assent from) our impressions, as I did when my wallet was stolen. Rather than reacting immediately to what another person is saying—which is never a good idea, as doing so will simply escalate a heated situation—we can slow down, rephrase what the other person is saying, take the time to analyze the possible underlying reasons, and only *then* respond. For example, you may interpret a request from your companion as an undue and irritating invasion of your personal space. But could it be that the request arises from your companion's need for more attention and care, a need that could be accommodated in some other way that would not make you feel like you have entered a prison?

The APA also counsels humor as an antidote to anger, and we have seen this deployed both by ancient Stoics like Epictetus (If I have to die now, then I die now; but if later, then now I'm going to dine, because it's dinnertime) and by modern ones like Irvine (Oh, you think that essay I wrote was fundamentally misguided? That's because you haven't read all my other essays!). However, the APA also rightly recommends using humor judiciously: we should neither simply laugh off our problems (or, worse, other people's) nor cross the fuzzy line between humor and sarcasm. Sarcasm, an aggressive and belittling type of response, is rarely useful, and certainly not in those situations that involve conflict and anger. But how do we tell the difference between humor and sarcasm? That takes practice as well as exercising the cardinal virtue of wisdom, which is precisely about learning how to navigate complex situations that have no clear line dividing black from white—like, you know, almost all of real life.

Additional suggestions from professional psychologists include changing your environment, for instance, by taking a physical break from the problematic situation; shifting the timing of your interaction with another person if the present moment seems not to be the best time to handle the problem, but being sure to set an alternative time for coming back to it in order to send the signal that you are not dodging it; practicing avoidance by not exposing yourself, if possible, to the cause of your distress; and finding alternative ways of doing what you need to do that may reduce the opportunity for conflict while still allowing you to accomplish your goals. We don't find all of these suggestions in the ancient Stoic texts, but they're all in synch with the fundamental Stoic idea that to live a good life we have to learn about how the world actually works (as opposed to how we wish it would work), and that we must also learn how to reason correctly in order to best handle the world as it is. Appreciating and using the pertinent findings of modern psychology to flourish in our lives, then, is a most Stoic thing to do.

EPICTETUS HAD A FEW INTERESTING THINGS TO TELL ME about anxiety as well. I used to be more anxious than I am now, a change that I attribute largely to experience (as it turns out, many things are not as bad as one imagines them to be before they happen) and a bit of the emotional maturity that is almost inevitable with the passing of the years and the changing of one's hormonal profile. But Epictetus helped me make an additional leap forward. He pointed out, for instance, that just as anger isn't usually very reasonable, neither is anxiety, and in fact both feelings can seriously get in the way of our projects and our quality of life.

Why are we so anxious about all sorts of things? "When I see a man in a state of anxiety, I say, 'What can this man want? If he did not want something which is not in his power, how could he still be anxious? It is for this reason that one who sings to the lyre is not anxious when he is performing by himself, but when he enters the theatre, even if he has a very good voice and plays well: for he not only wants to perform well, but also to win a great name, and that is beyond his own control.'" This is yet another version of Epictetus's cardinal idea of the dichotomy of control, but the way he puts it in this passage struck me as so obviously true, and so applicable to countless personal experiences, that my reaction was a loud "Duh! How could I have missed this?"

When I go, say, in front of a classroom full of students, I have no reason to be anxious, because I am well prepared to explain the material at hand. I'm a professional, I know what I'm doing, and I have a lot of experience with the subject matter—certainly much more than any of my students. The anxiety, then, is caused by an underlying fear of somehow disappointing the students, of not being sufficiently clear, entertaining, helpful, and so on. But the only way to avoid such failures is to do what I have already done: prepare myself to the best of my abilities. Nothing else can be done, so there is no cause for (additional) concern, much less for anxiety over the outcome. This, again, is not counsel to ignore or belittle my duties to my students. It is simply a reasonable reassessment of the situation I find myself in, in order to arrive at a useful distinction between the things that I should and should not be concerned about. Moreover, should I indeed "embarrass" myself in front of my class, what exactly is the worst thing that could happen? That some young people will laugh at my mistake, whatever it was? Worse things happen at sea, you know, as the Monty Python song goes.

Let me be clear that I am perfectly aware that some disorders of the mind may cause a type of anxiety that "cold hard logic," as the APA puts it, won't be able to overcome by itself. But those are *disorders*, that is, pathological conditions, for which modern psychology and psychiatry are beginning—however imperfectly—to provide remedies, in the form of both talk and pharmaceutical therapies. As my colleague Lou Marinoff put it in the preface to his best-selling book *Plato, Not Prozac!*, these therapies will accomplish the important, but insufficient, task of calming your mind to the point where you can be functional again. That by itself won't do the thinking for you, and it is a rethinking of a whole host of life's situations that promises to provide a path to eudaimonia.

That is why it is peculiar that people tend to pay attention to, and be worried by, exactly the wrong sort of things. Epictetus explained it to me this way: "We are anxious for our bit of a body, for our bit of property, for what Caesar will think, but are not anxious at all for what is within us. Am I anxious about not conceiving a false thought? No, for that depends on myself. Or about indulging an impulse contrary to nature? No, not about this either." The point here is more philosophical than psychological, of course; Epictetus is addressing the long-term course of our lives rather than whatever immediate problem we may face. But his point is crucial nonetheless. A religious person, putting it slightly differently, would speak in terms of taking care of one's soul rather than just one's body and possessions, but the idea is the same: we tend to adopt upside-down priorities, to be worried about things that are ultimately less important and definitely less under our control than what we should really be worried about and focusing energy and time on. Let Caesar (or your boss) think what he may—you yourself have to attend to the crucial task of improving your character and maintaining your integrity. If he is a good person, Caesar (or your boss) will appreciate it. If he is not, the loss, ultimately, is his no less than it was for the thief who stole Epictetus's lamp, and the one who lifted my wallet.

I live in a big city, and yet I spend most of the day on my own, reading and writing, either at home or in one of my two offices, both of which are usually devoid of colleagues or students. I spend my time this way by choice, and it suits my personality very well. But I couldn't help bringing up the issue of loneliness with Epictetus, since it seems to be a major one affecting modern society—not just the Western variety, and not only in big cities. It isn't difficult these days to find headlines that read: "The Loneliness Epidemic: We're More Connected Than Ever—But Are We Feeling More Alone?," "Is Modern Life Making Us Lonely?," "The Loneliness of American Society," and so forth.

A paper published by Colin Killeen in the *Journal of Advanced Nursing* offers an interesting discussion of loneliness from a modern, scientific perspective. To begin with, Killeen distinguishes loneliness from similar, yet separate, related concepts, such as alienation (which may be the result, or in some cases the cause, of depression) and solitude (which actually has a positive connotation, more akin to my own behavior). Interestingly, the paper presents a classification of what Killeen calls the "alienation-connectedness continuum" from negative to positive—alienation <> loneliness <> social isolation <> aloneness <> solitude <> connectedness—with society's perspective ranging from negative at the alienation extreme to positive at the connectedness one. The author superimposes on this continuum what he calls a "choice continuum"—from no choice (alienation, loneliness) at one extreme to total choice (solitude, connectedness) at the other. This choice continuum, of course, pertains to external causes of loneliness, not to internal attitudes, which are more within the proper domain of Stoic thought.

What are the causes of loneliness? The Killeen paper provides a handy summary diagram identifying a series of causes related to our situations and our characters that lead to loneliness, including bereavement, psychological vulnerability, reduced social network, depression, and radical life changes. These are accompanied by a number of associated factors, including age, gender, and health. The bottom line, in Killeen's view, is that there is no "solution" to the problem of loneliness, because it is highly multifactorial and because it depends on both personal (psychological, situational) and structural (societal) factors. What then? Here is the author's surprisingly sober yet refreshingly honest commentary: "[Loneliness] is such an innate part of the human psyche, that it cannot be solved like a puzzle; it can only be alleviated and made less painful. This can only be achieved by increasing humankind's awareness of this distressing condition that everyone has to endure in some way, shape or form, sometime during their lives, about which there is nothing to be embarrassed."

Those words resonate for me in part because they force-fully remind me of Epictetus's advice on the same subject: "The forlorn state is the condition of one without help. For a man is not forlorn simply because he is alone, any more than a man in a crowd is unforlorn. For according to its conception the term 'forlorn' means that a man is without help, exposed to those who wish to harm him. But nevertheless a man must prepare himself for solitude too—he must be able to suffice for himself, and able to commune with himself." As Killeen says: there is no reason to be embarrassed because (some de-gree of) loneliness is a natural condition for humanity, and Stoics reject the whole idea of embarrassment, especially with respect to societal expectations, because we have no influence over other people's judgments, only over our own behavior. Notice also Killeen's use of the word "endure," which is very much what Epictetus is talking about.

One distinction between loneliness and being alone would have been perfectly clear to the Stoics: the latter is a factual description, while the former is a judgment we superimpose on that description, and it is that judgment, not the naked fact, that makes us feel rejected and powerless. Importantly, however, there is a positive message in Epictetus's words, which can seem rather stern at first glance: the other side of endurance is resilience, and resilience is empowering. We may have little or no control over the external circumstances that force us into being alone at some times in our lives. But (save for pathological conditions, for which one needs to seek medical help), it is our choice, our own attitude, that turns solitude into loneliness. We may be alone, but we do not consequently need to feel helpless.

CHAPTER 13

LOVE AND FRIENDSHIP

Whoever then has knowledge of good things, would know how to love them; but how could one who cannot distinguish good things from evil and things indifferent from both have power to love?

—EPICTETUS, *DISCOURSES*, II.22

ONE DAY A DISTRAUGHT FATHER CAME TO SEEK EPICTETUS'S counsel. His daughter was terribly ill, and he simply couldn't stand it any longer, so he ran from the house in pain: "I am so miserable about my poor children, that lately when my daughter was ill and was thought to be in danger I could not bear to be near her, but fled away from her, until someone brought me news that she was well."

"Well, do you think you were right to do it?"

"It was natural, all fathers, or most of us, at least, feel like that."

Epictetus engaged the distraught father at length, because the Stoics made a big deal of "following nature," by which, however, they did not mean just doing whatever comes "naturally"—like leaving your own child in the care of others because you are experiencing too much pain. Epictetus told the man that he didn't deny that many fathers felt like he did, or that it was a natural way for fathers to feel. The question, though, was whether it was right. So he proceeded in classical Socratic fashion: "Was it right, I ask, for you, being affectionately disposed to your child, to run away and leave her? Is her mother not fond of the child?"

"She is indeed."

"Should the mother then have left her too, or should she not?"

"She should not."

"What of the nurse? Is she fond of the child?"

"She is."

"Ought she then to have left her?"

"By no means."

"Again, is not the child's attendant fond of her?"

"He is."

"Ought he then to have gone away and left her? Was it right that as a consequence the child should be thus left desolate and helpless because of the great affection of you its parents and of those about it, or should die in the hands of those who had no love or care for it?"

"Heaven forbid!"

"Tell me, would you have liked, if you were ill, your relations and everyone else, even your wife and children, to show their affection for you in such a way as to leave you alone and desolate?"

"Certainly not!"

"Would you pray to be so loved by your own people, as to be always left alone by them when you were ill, because of their exceeding affection, or would you, if it were a question of being left alone, rather pray, supposing that were possible, to have the affection of your enemies?"

You see where this is going. And yet many people misunderstand what Epictetus, and the Stoics more generally, were up to here. Sure, we can follow his undeniable logic, but isn't he saying that a father's love for his daughter boils down to duty? And isn't that a rather sterile, even inhuman, view of love and affection?

It would be, if that superficial reading of the anecdote reflected what Epictetus actually meant, but it doesn't—far from it. The point, rather, is that human affection needs to be guided—trained even—by a sound assessment of whatever situation triggers our feelings. It is undeniably true that the father should not have left his daughter just to avoid being in pain himself. This is elegantly shown by Epictetus, both by way of making the parallel between the father and his daughter's other caretakers—in comparison to whom he clearly behaved badly—and by asking the man to consider for a minute whether he himself, had he been in the place of his daughter, would have appreciated similar behavior from a loved one.

But that's only half of the Stoic point: there is a difference between what is natural and what is right, and we ought to arrive at correct judgments that will sometimes make us override what is natural in favor of what is right. This point derives from the Stoic theory of *oikeiôsis*, which we have already encountered in the form of Hierocles's widening (or, to be precise, contracting) circles of concern. The idea is that we begin life with only instinctual behaviors, some of which are rather selfish, just like the father's "natural" reaction to his daughter's pain. Once we enter the age of reason in mid-childhood, however, we begin to be able to reflect on things and to separate natural from good when necessary. But this isn't just a matter of letting "cold" reason take over our emotions. It doesn't work that way, and if the Stoics had really advocated such a simplistic notion, they'd have been really poor psychologists—which they most definitely were not.

Epictetus once told his students: "But though we are capable of writing and reading these sentiments, though we can praise them as we read, yet they do not bring conviction to us, nor anything like it. Wherefore the proverb about the Lacedaemonians, Lions at home, foxes at Ephesus, will fit us too. In the lecture-room we are lions, and foxes in the world outside!" What he meant was that simply recognizing the truth of something is not enough: you need to practice it, over and over, until you develop a habit that incorporates a rational conclusion into your instinctual repertoire. Think of practicing philosophy in the same way you learn to drive a car, or to kick a soccer ball, or to play the saxophone. Initially, it's all about paying conscious attention to what you're doing, and asking why, and as a result you are pretty bad at it, constantly making mistakes and getting frustrated. But little by little, the repetition of deliberate movements makes your actions more and more automatic, until it becomes second nature to hit the brakes when someone unexpectedly crosses the street, to pass the ball to your teammate who is suddenly unguarded by the other team's defense, or to hit the right sequence of notes at the right pace to produce the melody you want out of your instrument. True philosophy is a matter of a little theory and a lot of practice: "We see that the carpenter becomes a carpenter by learning certain things, the helmsman becomes a helmsman by learning certain things. May we, then, infer that in the sphere of conduct too it is not enough merely to wish to become good, but one must learn certain things? . . . For it is not arguments that are wanting nowadays: no, the books of the Stoics are full of them. What then is the one thing wanting? We want the man who will apply his arguments, and bear witness to them by action."

Despite Epictetus's (right) emphasis on practice, the ancient Greeks actually developed a sophisticated theoretical understanding of love, espousing a number of different conceptions of it, some of which are pertinent to the second subject of this chapter: friendship. Typically, scholars distinguish among *agápe*, *éros*, *philía*, and *storgē*. *Agápe* refers to the sort of love that you feel for your spouse and children, and that later on Christians associated with God's love for all humanity: as Thomas Aquinas put it, *agápe* is to will the good of another. If you think you know what *éros* means, you may have to think again. Yes, the word does carry the overt meaning of sensual pleasure and sexual attraction, but, as Plato explained in the Symposium, *éros* develops into an appreciation of the inner beauty of a person, through which we express our admiration for beauty itself, regardless of its specific incarnation. *Philía* is the dispassionate, virtuous love that we feel for friends, family, and community because we see and treat them as equal to ourselves. Finally, *storgē*, a far less frequently used word, specifically refers to love for your children but also, interestingly, for your country or sports team. It carries the meaning of an inherently felt love that has nothing to do with reason or reflection.

It is hard to deny that the single English word "love" simply doesn't quite catch all of these nuances, which is unfortunate, since we surely ought to distinguish the love we feel toward our partners, children, and friends from what we feel for, say, our country and God. In all cases, however, the Stoic question would be the very same one that Epictetus posed to the distraught father: it may be natural, but is it right?

We are often told, for instance, that we should love our country, "right or wrong," or our sports team regardless of whether they win or lose. I presume that both would be a *storgē* type of love, but a Stoic would argue that loving something "right or wrong" applies differently to the two cases. Indeed, that famous phrase has two sources, one derived from the other, that can be used to see why the Stoics were correct in saying that some kinds of love—the important ones—need to be squared with what is right, not just with our feelings about the matter. The original attribution of the quote is to Stephen Decatur, a US naval officer who allegedly said in an after-dinner toast in 1816: "Our Country! In her intercourse with foreign nations may she always be in the right; but right or wrong, our country!" Compare this with the derivative version, attributed to US Secretary of the Interior Carl Schurz, who used it in remarks before the Senate on February 29, 1872: "My country, right or wrong; if right, to be kept right; and if wrong, to be set right."

I submit that the Decatur version is more appropriate for a sports team: "AS Roma! In her intercourse with other teams may she always be victorious; but winner or loser, AS Roma!" There is something charming in harmless loyalty to a sports team, regardless, and in fact especially, if they tend to be on the losing side. But blind allegiance to your country can be—and historically has been, countless times—extremely dangerous. Indeed, I'm not aware of whether Schurz ever read Epictetus, but the US secretary essentially made the same point the philosopher did with the story of the distraught father: yes, it is understandable, and even commendable, to have certain natural feelings for our offspring or country. But since we are talking about human beings and foreign policy, respectively, not about sports teams, reason ought to be called in to guide us in our actions: I may *feel* like fleeing the house because I can't bear to see my daughter in pain, but the right thing to do is to stand by her and support her. I may *feel* like my country is a crucial part of my identity, which therefore justifies my having special regard for it, but if it is about to engage in actions that are deleterious to itself or to others, then I have a duty to speak out. If something really matters, feelings and reason cannot be decoupled and the latter promptly ignored.

SINCE FRIENDSHIP IS A TYPE OF LOVE, ACCORDING TO THE Greco-Romans, it is natural that it receives the same Stoic treatment from Epictetus as family relations:

> For where else is friendship but where faith and honour are, where men give and take what is good, and nothing else? "But he has paid me attention all this time: did he not love me?" How do you know, slave, whether he has paid you this attention, as a man cleans his boots, or tends

his beast? How do you know whether, when you have lost
your use as a paltry vessel, he will not throw you away like
a broken plate? . . . Were not Eteocles and Polynices born
of the same mother and the same father? Were they not
reared together, did they not live together, drink together,
sleep together, often kiss one another, so that if one had
seen them he would, no doubt, have laughed at the paradoxes of philosophers on friendship. Yet when the bit of
meat, in the shape of a king's throne, fell between them,
see what they say:

> E. Where wilt stand upon the tower?
> P. Wherefore dost thou ask me this?
> E. I will face thee then and slay thee.
> P. I desire thy blood no less.
> —EURIPIDES, THE PHOENISSAE, 621

Okay, the Master went poetic on me, and besides, Eteocles and Polynices were brothers, not just friends, but his
point is well taken: true friendship, like true love, is revealed
when the going gets tough, not when things are nice and easy.

From a Stoic perspective, friendship, like everything else
except our own moral character, is a preferred indifferent. This
raises interesting questions, since it means, for instance, that
there cannot be any such thing as (Stoic) friendship between
criminals, if "criminal" refers not just to someone wanted by
the law (after all, Nelson Mandela was a criminal from the
point of view of the South African apartheid government),
but to a person who engages in despicable acts of violence or
thievery. This is true not only because it is rather difficult to

imagine a virtuous criminal, but also because every time a criminal helps his criminal friend with, say, getting away with escaping justice, he puts his friendship for the other ahead of moral integrity—precisely the reverse of the Stoic set of priorities.

The same problem applies to love, both toward our relatives and toward our companion. The world's literature (including Greco-Roman literature) is full of stories of people putting love above everything else, leading on occasion to rather nasty consequences for themselves, the other person, or innocent third parties. But we are often encouraged to admire these individuals, because, after all, "love conquers all." Besides the fact that "love conquers all" only in a highly Disneyfied world, the Stoics would simply say that those are not cases of true friendship or true love, precisely because they show "friendship" and "love" trumping a person's moral character. We have already encountered Medea, who, before she went completely mad and killed her own children in revenge against her unfaithful husband, Jason, betrayed her father and killed her brother in order to help Jason steal the legendary Golden Fleece—allegedly, out of love for him. According to the Stoics, whatever it was that Medea felt for Jason, that sentiment wasn't really love. And neither is what is often labeled the same way in plenty of contemporary everyday news stories that are just as horrifying as the ancient tale of Medea.

Now, one could reasonably suspect that the Stoics were up to semantic tricks when they maintained that what many people consider friendship or love are in fact no such thing. But that would be to miss the point: the Stoics were both keen observers of human psychology (a descriptive activity) and sophisticated thinkers about human morality (a prescriptive activity). They would have easily granted that Medea felt what is commonly described as "love" toward Jason, or that, say, two Mafia bosses may be "friends" according to standard parlance. But they would have added, on the strength of their understanding of ethics, that these are the wrong words to describe what is going on in these cases. Why does this matter? Because if we use "love" and "friendship" to describe both situations in which morality is trumped and situations in which it is central, then we confuse things by not making semantic distinctions where there are substantive differences. "It's just semantics" is a weird dismissal of sometimes necessary clarifications of language, because our ability to communicate with and understand each other depends on semantics—that is, on our accurate use of language.

Let me give you an example from Aristotle, who was definitely not a Stoic. (Seneca, certainly a Stoic, used to help himself to the thoughts of the rival school of Epicurus, arguing that truth is the property of everyone, regardless of where it comes from, so I'm simply following his lead here.) Aristotle was arguably a bit obsessed with taxonomies; for instance, he proposed a whopping twelve different types of virtue rather than the Stoics' simple four, even though all types of virtue are really just different aspects of wisdom. When it comes to friendship, Aristotle focused in particular on *philía*, which, we have seen, refers to relations not just with those whom we today would call friends but also with close family—that's why it's not strange that Epictetus brings up the story of the brothers Eteocles and Polynices in his discussion of friendship. Aristotle distinguished among three types of friendship that I think still provide a useful framework today: friendship of utility, friendship of pleasure, and friendship of the good.

A friendship of utility is what we nowadays would call an acquaintance based on reciprocal advantage—say, for instance, your relationship with your favorite hairdresser. My mother used to run such a shop for many years in Rome, and it was clear from even a casual observation that her relationship with her clients was not just one of business. These women spent a significant amount of time, over prolonged periods of their lives, having their hair or other aesthetic work, like nails and such, done by my mother and her assistants. While the work was professionally attended to, there was much talk about all sorts of things, ranging from personal affairs to politics. (I don't remember much philosophy being discussed, though.) This certainly didn't make my mother a "friend" of the women in her parlor in the strict sense of the term, but it did make her more than just an anonymous person with whom they simply made business transactions. The ancients' idea was a good one: even though the relationship is largely established on mutual practical benefit and may terminate as soon as such benefit is exhausted, we still want to behave cordially and have positive social intercourse with other human beings, since it is the right and pleasurable thing to do—right because we are treating others as ends in themselves, not just as means to our ends, as Kant would have put it; and pleasurable because we are by nature social beings who derive satisfaction from talking to other social beings.

A "friendship of pleasure," the second Aristotelian category of *philía*, is rather obviously based on (again, reciprocal) pleasure. Think of your drinking buddies, or people with whom you share a hobby. Like friendship of utility, this one too is based on mutual advantage, only this time the advantage is not instrumental but pleasurable. Just as with friendships of utility, friendships of pleasure don't need to be deep, though in modern English usage we would probably deploy the word "friend" rather than "acquaintance" in these cases. And of course, like friendships of utility, friendships of pleasure may also end once the pertinent social glue dissolves—for instance, because we lose interest in a particular hobby, or discover a new watering hole in a different part of town.

The third category of Aristotelian friendship goes well beyond the minimal requirements that most people would expect to be met before calling someone a friend: a friendship of the good is that rare phenomenon when two people enjoy each other for their own sake because they find in each other an affinity of character that does not require externalities like a business exchange or a hobby. In those cases, our friends become, as Aristotle famously put it, mirrors to our souls, helping us grow and become better persons just because they care about us. Again, you can see why "friendship of the good" may refer not just to friendships in the modern sense of the term but also to relationships with family members or with our companion.

Once more, Aristotle was no Stoic, and the Stoics would have said that the only friendship that truly deserves to be called a friendship is that of the good. Crucially, however, they would not have denied either the existence or the importance of the other two classes. But they would have confined them to the category of "preferred indifferents": things you may very well have and cultivate, so long as they don't interfere with your virtues and moral integrity.

It is noteworthy that the Greco-Roman categorizations of types of love and friendship are not just much richer than our own, but also somewhat differently organized conceptually: they associated aspects of relationships that we keep distinct, as when we differentiate "friends" (of one type) from family members (of another type) from business acquaintances. In the end, concepts, and the words that allow us to deploy them, are useful insofar as they help us navigate the realities of our world, especially our social environment. But it will come as no surprise to the reader that I admire the ancients' rich vocabulary in this respect and would suggest that perhaps we lost something significant when we pared down our own language. After all, a meaningfully richer language reflects a more nuanced thinking and a better ability to negotiate existence.

CHAPTER 14

PRACTICAL SPIRITUAL EXERCISES

> Admit not sleep into your tender eyelids till you have reckoned up each deed of the day—How have I erred, what done or left undone? So start, and so review your acts, and then for vile deeds chide yourself, for good be glad.

—EPICTETUS, *Discourses*, III.10

WE HAVE TALKED ENOUGH WITH EPICTETUS, I THINK, TO have a good grasp of what Stoicism is about, both in theory and as practically applied to everyday life, whether in the Roman Empire in the second century BCE or now during the twenty-first century. How, then, are we supposed to actually experience Stoicism as a living philosophy?

There is no single way, nor is there a fixed set of doctrines resembling anything like a religious catechism to go by—which I think is an unqualified positive. But there are people—such as myself and the authors of a number of other recent books on Stoicism—who have developed a practice based on a combination of what is actually found in ancient texts, modern techniques derived from cognitive behavioral and similar therapies, and just what does and does not work for us individually. Different approaches to Stoicism work better for different people, so it is best to treat the advice that follows as a set of suggestions, not as rigid rules to stick to no matter what.

Naturally, I consulted Epictetus himself, and he directed me to his *Enchiridion*, which literally means "handbook." Of course, he didn't write the book (as far as we know, he didn't write anything, really); the *Enchiridion* was put together by Arrian of Nicomedia. Now, I'm not sure how comfortable I would feel if my only legacy to humanity was a bunch of notes on my lectures taken by one of my students, but some students are brighter than others, and at any rate, this is what we have from Epictetus. Naturally, our legacy is yet another thing we do not control, though we have control over how we interpret and use someone else's.

Then again, Arrian wasn't just your average student, even for the times. He became a well-known historian, a military commander, and a public servant of the Roman Empire, being elected Consul in 130 CE, then Prefect of the Province of Cappadocia. Arrian probably attended Epictetus's school between 117 and 120 CE, then remained attached to his Master in Nicopolis for a while. Arrian eventually left for Athens, and subsequently embarked on a distinguished career, which included being appointed senator by Emperor Hadrian. When he retired, Arrian went back to Athens, where he became Archon, or chief magistrate (apparently he couldn't just stand still and do nothing). He died during the reign of Marcus Aurelius, the Stoic emperor. The poet Lucian of Samosata wrote that Arrian was "a Roman of the first rank with a lifelong attachment to learning." Having notes on my lectures taken by that sort of student would, I think, be more than acceptable.

I have gone through the *Enchiridion*, compiled by Arrian on the basis of Epictetus's lectures, and distilled twelve "spiritual exercises," or Stoic reminders of how to act in everyday life. The best way to begin using them, I think, would be to attach to your calendar a handy list of them, in no particular order. (They are presented here simply in the sequence in which they appear in the *Enchiridion*.) These days there are plenty of apps for smart phones and the like that will easily allow you to do this. Set up the list in such a way that you'll be reminded of one of these practices every day, in rotation (or, to make things more interesting, at random). Each day reread Epictetus's words several times, whenever you have a minute, and focus on putting into practice that day a specific piece of advice. The first goal is to become mindful of the Stoic way to think and—most importantly—act. Eventually, the exercises should become so second nature that you won't need the reminders (though I still have them pop up on my calendar, just in case) and will be able to practice them spontaneously, applying them to all the small and big events and situations of your life.

The exercises that follow naturally make the most sense when understood through the lens of Stoic philosophy. So before discussing the exercises themselves, let me recap some of the fundamental principles of Stoicism we have learned throughout the book.

We have encountered a number of Stoic ideas during our conversations with Epictetus, beginning most importantly with the three Stoic disciplines—desire, action, and assent—and their relationship with the three areas of study—physics, ethics, and logic—as discussed in Chapter 2. (This may be a good time to go back to that discussion and refresh your understanding of these disciplines and areas of study.) The disciplines have been the logical backbone for the entire sequence of chapters in this book. Distilled to their bare minimum (in order to derive the most benefit from these spiritual exercises), the Stoic principles are as follows:

1. *Virtue is the highest good, and everything else is indifferent.* The Stoics got the first part from Socrates, who argued that virtue is the chief good because it is the only thing that is valuable under all circumstances and that helps us make proper use of things like health, wealth, and education. Everything else is indifferent in the specifically Stoic sense that nothing is to be traded against virtue. The Stoic can pursue the preferred indifferents and try to stay away from the dispreferred ones, so long as doing so doesn't interfere with virtue. In modern economic theory, this well-known approach is called a system of lexicographic preferences. To illustrate, you have a lexicographic preference if you wouldn't trade your daughter for a Lamborghini, no matter how much you'd love to have a Lamborghini.

2. *Follow nature.* That is, apply reason to social life. The Stoics thought that we should take a hint from how the universe is put together in figuring out how to live our lives. Since human beings are naturally social animals capable of reason, it follows that we should strive to apply reason to achieve a better society.

3. *Dichotomy of control.* Some things are under our control, and others are not (though we may be able to influence them). If we are sufficiently healthy mentally, our decisions and behaviors are under our control. Outside of our control is everything else. We should concern ourselves with what is under our control and handle everything else with equanimity.

Moreover, while engaging in the exercises proposed here, remember that they are supposed to further your mastery of the four Stoic virtues:

(Practical) wisdom: Navigating complex situations in the best available fashion

Courage: Doing the right thing, both physically and morally, under all circumstances

Justice: Treating every human being—regardless of his or her stature in life—with fairness and kindness

Temperance: Exercising moderation and self-control in all spheres of life

Now that we have reviewed the basic principles underlying the Stoic system, we are better equipped to examine (and put into practice!) the twelve exercises I extracted from Epictetus's (well, actually, Arrian's) *Enchiridion*:

1. Examine your impressions. "So make a practice at once of saying to every strong impression: 'An impression is all you are, not the source of the impression.' Then test and assess it with your criteria, but one primarily: ask, 'Is this something that is, or is not, in my control?' And if it's not one of the things that you control, be ready with the reaction, 'Then it's none of my concern.'"

This is the classic dichotomy of control with which we began this book. Epictetus exhorts us to practice what is arguably the most fundamental of his doctrines: to constantly examine our "impressions"—that is, our initial reactions to events, people, and what we are being told—by stepping back to make room for rational deliberation, avoiding rash emotional reactions, and asking whether whatever is being thrown at us is under our control (in which case we should act on it) or isn't (in which case we should regard it as not of our concern).

For instance, a few days before writing this I got food poisoning (from spoiled fish) and experienced a pretty bad forty-eight hours, during which I could hardly do anything interesting, let alone work and write. Ordinarily, this would be something "bad," an experience that most of us might be inclined to complain about and seek sympathy for. The biochemistry of my body and of potentially pathogenic agents, however, is most definitely not under my control (though deciding to eat fish at that particular restaurant certainly was). So it made no sense for me to complain about being sick with food poisoning, since I could not change what had already happened. And though it is certainly human to seek sympathy, even that response—from a Stoic perspective—is an imposition on others in order to feel better ourselves, in a situation in which, moreover, others cannot do much more than pity us. It is perfectly acceptable for a Stoic to sympathize with others, but it seems a bit self-centered to *require* sympathy from others when we are sick ourselves. Instead, I acted in accordance with Epictetus's words: I accepted what was happening as a fact of biology, took the medical precautions that seemed to be in order (taking some probiotics), and then adjusted my mental attitude to my predicament. I couldn't work or write. Well, then, I would not even try, since there were other things I could do instead, and at any rate I was very likely to recover quickly, after which there would be plenty of time to work and write.

One last comment here: the "it's none of my concern" bit is often misunderstood. The idea isn't that we should not care about what is happening to us. During my bout of food poisoning, for instance, I was forcefully reminded that health is ranked by the Stoics as a preferred indifferent—something that is to be sought unless it compromises our integrity and virtue. But if there truly is nothing more to be done about a given situation, then we should no longer "concern" ourselves with it—we should stop trying to do something about the situation—precisely *because* it is outside of our control. Larry Becker calls this the "axiom of futility," which he spells out in rather crisp terms: "Agents are required not to make direct attempts to do (or be) something that is logically, theoretically, or practically impossible." Wise words, it seems to me.

2. **Remind yourself of the impermanence of things.** "In the case of particular things that delight you, or benefit you, or to which you have grown attached, remind yourself of what they are. Start with things of little value. If it is china you like, for instance, say, 'I am fond of a piece of china.' When it breaks, then you won't be as disconcerted. When giving your wife or child a kiss, repeat to yourself, 'I am kissing a mortal.' Then you won't be so distraught if they are taken from you."

This very famous passage from the *Enchiridion* shocks students when they first hear it. It is one of the most misinterpreted bits of Stoic wisdom, sometimes even willfully so. That is why it is all the more important that we understand it properly. The troublesome part, of course, is not what Epictetus says about the piece of china, but the part that follows concerning one's wife or child. If Epictetus had stopped at the first example, I think we would have all taken this to be a reasonable reminder not to get attached to *things*, perhaps even a second-century warning against consumerism. (Consumerism is not a modern American invention; there was plenty of it going around at the time of the Roman Empire—for those, then as now of course, who could actually afford to consume.) The second part, however, reveals a truly deep insight into the human condition, and may require some background to be properly appreciated. After all, Stoicism was thought of by its practitioners as a philosophy of love—not of callous disregard for human beings and their sufferings.

First off, let's remind ourselves of the historical context: Epictetus was writing at a time when even emperors (like Marcus Aurelius himself) lost most of their children and other loved ones at what we would consider a tender or premature age, to disease, random violence, or war. While most of us in the West and in a few other parts of the world are currently lucky in that respect (especially if we happen to be white and male), it remains true today that life is ephemeral, and people we deeply care about may be snatched from us suddenly and without warning.

Second, and more crucially, what Epictetus is counseling here is not an inhuman indifference toward our beloved ones, but quite the opposite: we should constantly remind ourselves of just how precious our loved ones are precisely because they may soon be gone. Anyone who has lost someone they were close to ought to know exactly what this means. The idea is that we should go through life just as the Roman generals did during official celebrations of their triumphs in the Eternal City: with somebody constantly whispering in our ear, "Memento homo" (Remember, you are only a man).

Forgive me if, again, I make this personal. I lost my mother to cancer at about the time I was beginning to study Stoicism seriously. I had lost my father to the same disease (and probably because of the same triggering factor, smoking) a decade earlier. Both those losses affected me deeply, not because I had had an idyllic relationship with either of my parents (I hadn't, and instead feel most indebted to my paternal grandmother and her partner, my adoptive grandfather, with whom I grew up), but because they marked the passing of the very two individuals who brought me into this world. Losing one's parents is a rite of passage for most of us (unless we happen to die before them), and anyone who has gone through the experience will testify to how hard it is, regardless of the specific circumstances. Yet I observed that the way I handled the illness and subsequent death of each of my parents was very different in the two instances.

When my father was diagnosed with the first of what turned out to be a number of distinct types of cancer, I simply did not take seriously the idea that I was going to have only a few more chances to spend some time with him—not only because of the suddenly shortened time horizon (he died at age sixty-nine), but also because we were living almost 7,000 kilometers apart, he in Rome and I in New York. I kept behaving as if we had all the time in the world and quite simply refused to internalize what my mind knew very well: what was happening was probably going to kill my father in a short time. It ended up taking about five years, but I still managed to be caught unaware by his final decline; as a result, I was not there when he finally died. (I was en route to the New York airport to take the flight for Rome.)

I always regretted the way I responded to my father's illness—until Stoicism taught me that regret is about things we can no longer change and the right attitude is to *learn* from our experiences, not dwell on decisions that we are not in a position to alter. Which brings me to my mother. Her demise was actually faster, and we didn't even realize what was happening for a while because of an initial misdiagnosis. But once the picture became clear, I was able to return to Italy and visit her with full awareness—and acceptance—of what was going on. Every time I left her at the hospital, after having kissed her good-bye, Epictetus's words rang comfortingly true. I really did not know whether I would see her the following day. None of this made the experience any less hard, since Stoicism isn't a magic wand. But I tried my best to be present in the *hic et nunc,* the here and now, as the Romans used to say. That mindfulness is what Epictetus is attempting to instill in his students: far from counseling us not to care (despite the "you won't be so distraught" of the English translation, which inevitably loses some of the poignancy of the original Greek), he is advising us to care and appreciate very much what we now have, precisely because Fate may snatch it from us tomorrow.

3. The reserve clause. "Whenever planning an action, mentally rehearse what the plan entails. If you are heading out to bathe, picture to yourself the typical scene at the bathhouse—people splashing, pushing, yelling and pinching your clothes. You will complete the act with more composure if you say at the outset, 'I want a bath, but at the same time I want to keep my will aligned with nature' [that is, to apply reason to social living]. Do it with every act. That way if something occurs to spoil your bath, you will have ready the thought, 'Well, this was not my only intention, I also meant to keep my will in line with nature—which is impossible if I go all to pieces whenever anything bad happens.'"

I love the "which is impossible if I go all to pieces whenever anything bad happens" bit. It conjures an image of people who are too fragile to withstand even minor challenges in life because they let themselves be fragile. They always assume that *of course* things will go well, since bad things only happen to other people (possibly because they somehow deserve them). Instead, as Stoics, we should bring the reserve clause to anything we do, and even use it as a personal mantra: Fate permitting.

Notice again that Epictetus here begins with a very simple situation: he wants to go to the baths and enjoy the experience. Just as we may want to go to the movies, say, and be able to watch the film without the glare of cell phones being lit up by obnoxious people who just *have* to check their messages one more time or else. Here too I speak from personal experience of course: I used to get really mad when this happened, and would occasionally engage the offender in a loud argument that, predictably, went nowhere. These days I react by deploying two of the Stoic techniques we have seen so far: First, of course, I think of the dichotomy of control. Going to the movies is under my control (I could, after all, watch another film at home or do something else entirely), and so is my reaction to other people's behaviors. And though the latter are certainly not under my control, I can influence them: by politely explaining to another movie patron why what he or she is doing is inconsiderate, or by going to the movie house's management and—again calmly and politely—complaining about the situation, since it is their responsibility to ensure that paying customers have an enjoyable experience while frequenting their establishment.

The second technique to deploy is the reserve clause, properly understood. Once more, Epictetus is not counseling us to passively accept other people's rudeness, but rather reminding us that we may set out with a particular goal in mind but that events may not go the way we wish. That being the case, our choices are to make ourselves miserable, thereby willfully worsening our situation, or to remember our overarching goal: to be a decent person who doesn't do anything that is unvirtuous or that may compromise our integrity (like behaving obnoxiously in reaction to another's obnoxious behavior).

There is a nice analogy in Stoic lore meant to explain the point. It is attributed to Chrysippus—the third head of the original Stoa of Athens—and was allegedly recounted in one of Epictetus's lost volumes of the *Discourses*. Imagine a dog who is leashed to a cart. The cart begins to move forward, in whatever direction the driver, but certainly not the dog, chooses. Now, the leash is long enough that the dog has two options: either he can gingerly follow the general direction of the cart, over which he has no control, and thereby enjoy the ride and even have time to explore his surroundings and attend to some of his own business, or he can stubbornly resist the cart with all his might and end up being dragged, kicking and screaming, for the rest of the trip, accumulating much pain and frustration and wasting his time in a futile and decidedly unpleasant effort. We humans are, of course, the dog: the universe keeps churning according to God's will (if you have religious inclinations) or cosmic cause and effect (if your taste is more secular). But you do have some room to maneuver, while you are alive and well, and can choose to enjoy the ride, even as you remain aware of the constraints you have and know that whatever you wish to accomplish always comes with a big caveat: Fate (the cart driver, God, the universe) permitting. This is what it means to do whatever you do while "keeping in line with nature."

There is yet another way to interpret the message of this exercise, and I thank my friend Bill Irvine for expressing it particularly clearly in his book *A Guide to the Good Life: The Ancient Art of Stoic Joy*. Let's suppose that you are playing a tennis match or, more consequentially, being considered for a promotion at your job. The Stoic approach to both situations is the one counseled by Epictetus, and one that Bill reinterprets as internalizing your goals. While we naturally think that our goal is to win the match, or get the promotion, those outcomes of course are not in our control—they can only be influenced by us. So we need to make our goal something that actually is in our power and not even Fate can rob us of: to play the best match we can, regardless of outcome, or to put together the best promotion file we can before the decision is made. By now I should not need to add the usual caveat, but *repetita iuvant* (repetition is helpful), as the Romans said: the idea is *not* to passively accept defeat in the tennis match, or perhaps absorb the injustice of not getting a promotion that was richly deserved. Rather, it is to deploy the wisdom that sometimes things will not go our way even if we do our best, and regardless of whether we deserved to win the match or get the promotion. Not to confuse one's aspirations, even well-grounded ones, with how the universe will (or ought to) act is one of the hallmarks of a wise person.

4. **How can I use virtue here and now?** "For every challenge, remember the resources you have within you to cope with it. Provoked by the sight of a handsome man or a beautiful woman, you will discover within you the contrary power of self-restraint. Faced with pain, you will discover the power of endurance. If you are insulted, you will discover patience. In time, you will grow to be confident that there is not a single impression that you will not have the moral means to tolerate."

I think of this passage as one of the most empowering of Stoic writings. Epictetus, the former slave, lame because of a once-broken leg, tells us to use every occasion, every challenge, as a way to exercise our virtue, to become a better human being by constant application. Notice how he counters each temptation or difficulty with a virtue that can be practiced, deploying the Stoic concept that every challenge in life is a perfectly good chance to work on self-improvement. When you see an attractive person walking by, you will not scheme to get that person in bed with you, unless both of you happen to be free from other relationships and pursuing your desires is not going to cause pain and suffering to others.

Rather, you will summon your self-control and focus on how you can alter your own mentality so that eventually you will simply not feel the temptation at all. The second example is of a different kind, and yet it evokes the same response in a Stoic, with a similar result: you cannot control disease and pain, and it will happen at some point or another in your life. But you can manage it, not just with medications (there is certainly nothing in Stoic doctrine that precludes the use of medicine when appropriate), but also by way of your own mental attitude. No wonder Epictetus is often associated with the phrase "bear and forbear," or "endure and renounce." But remember that the goal isn't to live an unhappy and grim life. On the contrary, it is to achieve what the Stoics called *apatheia*, which, despite the obvious and unappealing English echo, we have seen means tranquillity of mind, as well as equanimity toward whatever life happens to throw at us.

Here again, perhaps a personal anecdote will help. Not long ago I was home alone and preparing myself dinner, engaged in slicing an onion to sauté in preparation for a nice pasta meal. Unfortunately, the knife was rather blunt, it slipped, and I cut my left ring finger—deeply cut, as in, I had to hold it to prevent it from falling off. (At the moment of this writing, more than a year later, I still haven't completely regained sensation in that finger.) I distinctly remember automatically switching to an attitude that I probably would not have had a few years ago. I looked at what I had done, took the obvious precaution of holding the partly severed digit with my other hand, and then quickly decided that it wasn't going to be a good idea to wipe the blood off and that I should simply get out and walk to the nearby medical emergency facility to have them take care of my finger as best they could. On my way there I kept engaging in *premeditatio malorum* (foreseeing bad things): what was the worst thing that could happen, and how would I deal with it? I'm no medical doctor, but as far as I could tell, the worst-case scenario was going to involve a significant amount of pain, the loss of a bit of blood, and possibly the permanent loss of part of the finger. Well, that wasn't too bad, was it? I'm not a pianist, I'm pretty fast at typing my essays using mostly just two fingers, and such an outcome wouldn't change my appearance enough to create problems with my dating life. I could cope with it, I decided. And I did. Then things turned out significantly better than my *premeditatio* scenario allowed: I still have the full finger, and I even use it occasionally to help with the typing. My romantic life wasn't affected either, I'm happy to report.

5. Pause and take a deep breath. "Remember, it is not enough to be hit or insulted to be harmed, you must believe that you are being harmed. If someone succeeds in provoking you, realize that your mind is complicit in the provocation. Which is why it is essential that we not respond impulsively to impressions; take a moment before reacting, and you will find it is easier to maintain control."

As we have seen, Stoics handled insults very well, ideally like rocks. (Have you ever tried to insult a rock? How did it go?) Those who felt so inclined also responded with a sense of humor. The point here, however, is to practice the crucial step that allows us to more rationally examine our impressions, regardless of whether they are negative, such as insults, or positive such as feelings of lust: we need to resist the impulse to react immediately and instinctively to potentially problematic situations. Instead, we must pause, take a deep breath, perhaps go for a walk around the block, and only *then* consider the issue as dispassionately (in the sense of equanimity, not lack of care) as possible. This is simple advice, and yet it is very difficult to pull off. It is also very, very important. Once you start seriously practicing this exercise, you will see dramatic improvements in the way you handle things, and you'll get positive feedback from all the others who also see those improvements. I cannot even count, at this point, the number of occasions when doing what Epictetus says here saved a situation in my life *and* improved my mood.

You know the famous Nike commercial slogan, "Just Do It"? Well no, the Stoics disagree. If it is important, you really ought to stop and think about it before you decide *whether* to do it. Imagine how much less pain you would have inflicted on others, how many difficult or embarrassing situations you would have avoided, and just generally how much more self-confident and positive you would have felt if you had started doing this years ago. As our friend Epictetus puts it, "[The next time] you encounter anything troublesome or pleasant or glorious or inglorious, remember that the hour of struggle is come, the Olympic contest is here and you may put it off no longer, and that one day and one action determines whether the progress you have achieved is lost or maintained." The Olympic games of life have already started, and even if you did not join before, the time to join is now, not tomorrow.

6. Other-ize. "We can familiarize ourselves with the will of nature by calling to mind our common experiences. When a friend breaks a glass, we are quick to say, 'Oh, bad luck.' It's only reasonable, then, that when a glass of your own breaks, you accept it in the same patient spirit. Moving on to graver things: when somebody's wife or child dies, to a man we all routinely say, 'Well, that's part of life.' But if one of our own family is involved, then right away it's 'Poor, poor me!' We would do better to remember how we react when a similar loss afflicts others."

This exercise is a fascinating one: Epictetus reminds us here of just how differently we regard an event that has affected other people when the same event affects us. Naturally, it is far easier to maintain equanimity (which, again, is not to be confused with emotional impassivity!) when little inconveniences, or even disasters, happen to others rather than to ourselves. But why, really? What makes us think that we are the universe's special darlings, or that we ought to be?

Of course, even if we can bring ourselves to realize and internalize (which is far more difficult) that we are just like everyone else on the planet and should have the same attitude about an occurrence when it happens to others as when it happens to ourselves, we could still flip the argument on the Stoic and say that the right thing to do is to feel the same degree of pain and empathy for everyone's misfortunes as we do for our own. The Stoic has two responses to this argument—one based on empirical evidence, and the other from philosophical principles. The empirical fact is that human beings are simply incapable, physiologically, of that much empathy. To feel truly sorry and distraught for every life lost on planet Earth as we normally feel when our own loved ones die is, simply put, inhuman. The philosophical argument is that we are, if not entirely right, at least closer to the truth when we say to other people, "I'm truly sorry, but it is a fact of life," than when we tell ourselves, "Poor me! Poor me!" Accidents, injuries, disease, and death are unavoidable, and while it is understandable to be distraught over them (presumably in proportion to their gravity—breaking a glass is not the same thing as losing one's spouse!), we can take comfort in knowing that they are in the normal order of things. The universe isn't after anyone—or at least, it isn't after any one of us in particular!

I found both interpretations of the "other-ize" exercise useful in a number of recent experiences. Sometimes I tend to dismiss the feelings of people who are close to me on the grounds that they are overreacting to whatever is happening to them. But Epictetus reminds me that I tend to feel differently when similar things—like a cutting comment from a friend or a colleague—happen to me. By the same token, when it is my turn to be on the receiving end, I now instantly recall that pretty much everyone I know has experienced whatever it is that is upsetting me at the moment, or will experience it at some point in their lives. This constant habit of adjusting my own reactions to others' misfortunes and putting my problems in context by remembering that they are common to the broader humanity is—I think—gradually helping me see things with an equanimity that I definitely lacked before I got interested in Stoicism.

7. Speak little and well. "Let silence be your goal for the most part; say only what is necessary, and be brief about it. On the rare occasions when you're called upon to speak, then speak, but never about banalities like gladiators, horses, sports, food and drink—common-place stuff. Above all don't gossip about people, praising, blaming or comparing them."

I must admit that this is a hard one for me to practice, probably owing to my somewhat above-average ego and the professional habits of a teacher who is far too often in professorial mode. Still, I've tried to remember this counsel and take it to heart, and it is serving me increasingly well. Very few people wish to be lectured over dinner or on a social occasion. Come to think of it, probably very few people want to be lectured under any circumstances at all! So one side effect of this exercise is that it will probably make you more welcomed regardless of the occasion.

On closer inspection, Epictetus's list of things not to talk about is revealing in and of itself. We may not talk much these days about gladiators, but we do talk about star athletes, movie and music stars, and other "celebrities" (which, as a song from the musical *Chicago* aptly explains, means "to be famous for being famous"). Why should we refrain from such talk, or at least indulge in it as little as possible? Because it is fundamentally empty. Why should we care at all about what the Kardashians (or any other celebrities of the moment) are doing? To say that an interest in such matters is the hallmark of a rather shallow mind sounds elitist of course, and therefore distasteful to our modern sensibilities, but only because we have been conditioned to think that "serious" talk is boring and at any rate requires more background knowledge and attention than most of us associate with good conversation. This, however, has most definitely not always been true. Those who frequented ancient Greek symposia or their Roman equivalent, the *convivium* (which means "living together"), thought that a good dinner party hinged on involved discussions of philosophy, politics, and other "serious" matters. To make the discussion flow better, both the Greeks and the Romans served light wine and snacks. During the Enlightenment, private "salons" sprang up throughout Europe, and people competed to be invited to join in the salon conversations, with very few reports of ensuing boredom.

Epictetus's second list—the items of conversation we should stay away from "above all"—concerns gossip and judgments of people. This list requires some further discussion. Gossiping probably evolved over time as a way for people to "keep track," so to speak, of members of their tribe, which is very helpful when your survival depends on the trustworthiness (or not) of those around you. Although even in modern society we need to appraise the people with whom we interact in order to decide whether we can rely on them as life partners, friends, business associates, coworkers, and so forth, this is probably best done directly, in person, based on what the people in question actually say and—especially—on what they do. To indulge in gossip and judge people who are not present to defend themselves simply does not seem to be the virtuous thing to do, and the Stoic idea is that we debase ourselves whenever we engage in such activity.

An important part of what Epictetus is suggesting here builds on the general Stoic principle that we can decide on our best course of action and then redirect our behavior accordingly. Initially, this is difficult, and even feels unnatural, but then habit kicks in and redirecting our behavior becomes easier and easier—until we reach the point where we wonder how we could have ever behaved otherwise. So I don't suggest that you suddenly and drastically change your demeanor at social events. But give it a try and see how it fits you. Begin by responding less and less to talk of "gladiators" and such and occasionally introduce a more challenging topic of your own that is based on something you've recently read or watched and that you feel might lead to a mutually beneficial conversation with your friends. See what happens! I'm still surprised at how much more I enjoy dinner parties now.

8. Choose your company well. "Avoid fraternizing with non-philosophers. If you must, though, be careful not to sink to their level; because, you know, if a companion is dirty, his friends cannot help but get a little dirty too, no matter how clean they started out."

I laugh every time I read this, since it is yet another example of Stoic, shall we say, bluntness; it is bound to shock modern sensibilities, and yet, the more I reflect on it, the more I become convinced that modern sensibilities could benefit from the occasional shock. Indeed, to our ears this sort of advice sounds (again!) insufferably elitist, but only a moment's reflection reveals that it is not. First of all, remember the source: it comes from an ex-slave who was making a living teaching in the open air, not from a stuffy aristocrat living in a semi-secluded Roman version of a McMansion or a gated community. Second, realize that by "philosophers" Epictetus doesn't mean professional academics (trust me, you don't want to make a habit of socializing mostly with *them*), but rather people who are interested in following virtue and cultivating their character. From the ancient perspective, which we would do well to make our own, everyone ought to strive to be a philosopher in this sense of the term—that is, to apply reason to improve his own and his community's life and well-being. Even more generally, this is simply the sound advice that our life is short, temptation and waste are always lurking, and so we need to pay attention to what we are doing and who our companions are.

Again, I have tried to slowly implement this strategy in my own social interactions—it goes very well with the previous exercise of engaging in less and more meaningful conversation. I don't mean simply that I have cleaned up the roster of my Facebook "friends" (although I have done that too), but that I truly pay attention to whom I spend my time with and why. Ideally, remember how Aristotle (not a Stoic!) put it: we want to be with friends who are better than ourselves, so that we can learn from them. At the very least, we want our friends to be the sort of people who can hold up a mirror to our soul, so that we can look into it frankly and gain a better idea of just how much work needs to be done on it (the soul, not the mirror).

9. Respond to insults with humor. "If you learn that someone is speaking ill of you, don't try to defend yourself against the rumors; respond instead with, 'Yes, and he doesn't know the half of it, because he could have said more.'"

This is a lovely example of profound wisdom accompanied by Epictetus's own distinctive brand of humor: instead of getting offended by someone's insults (remember, what they say is not yours to control), respond with self-deprecation. You will feel better, and your vilifier will be embarrassed, or at the least disarmed. The already mentioned Bill Irvine has worked this advice into an art form. He tells the story of a colleague in his department who once stopped him in the middle of the hall to say, "I was just trying to decide whether to cite your work in my next paper." At first Bill was delighted, thinking that one of his own colleagues actually appreciated his technical work (believe me, it doesn't happen as often as you might think, especially in philosophy departments), but the colleague immediately went on: "Yes, but I can't decide if what you wrote is just misguided or downright evil." Now, most of us would be quite offended by that sort of comment, which may have been meant as either an "observation" without malice (academics have a not entirely undeserved reputation for being, shall we say, socially unaware) or in fact an intentional put-down. Rather than defend himself from the charge and launch into a detailed, and probably useless, explanation of why his paper was neither evil nor misguided, Bill did the Stoic thing: he took a breath, smiled, and replied: "Well, good thing you haven't read my other works, or you'd see just how evil *and* misguided I *really* am."

I'm sure the reader will have no trouble believing that this is advice that I have also tried, if imperfectly, to put into practice. Doing so has made a significant difference in the way I relate to others, especially hostile others. In my younger days, I was far more insecure and prone to take offense, sometimes brooding for hours, or even losing sleep, over what I perceived as an insult, especially if it had come from someone I admired or regarded as a friend. No more. Now I follow Bill and actually relish the occasions on which I receive insults (which are fairly rare, I must say).

The best arena to practice what he calls "insult pacifism" is, of course, the Internet. I maintain an active set of social networks for professional and outreach work, not to mention two blogs, and as I'm sure is common experience, that provides highly fertile ground for trolling, grandstanding, and general rudeness. I therefore had to set ground rules for my readers and followers—as well as for myself—very early on in the game, before I got interested in Stoicism. Since then, meeting insults with humor has most definitely made my virtual life a far more pleasant experience. First, however, I follow Epictetus's previous advice about speaking little and to the point: I simply do not respond or engage as much as I did before, while increasing the time I spend just listening. More importantly, I have begun to internalize the concept that an insult works, not because it is intended as such by the person who delivers it, but because the target allows it to become an insult.

There are two important caveats to discuss concerning this exercise. First and foremost, this shouldn't be taken as a backhanded way to ignore the serious problem of bullying, of both the cyber and in-person varieties. Bullying is a behavior that is not acceptable and ought to be nipped in the bud, especially when aimed—as it often is—at minors or at people who suffer from psychological issues that make them particularly susceptible to it. But this is true in general of a lot of what the Stoics advise: the two approaches—working on eliminating or curtailing a problem while at the same time developing one's own endurance—are simply not mutually exclusive. As a matter of fact, not only is there no need to choose one strategy or the other, but they can be reciprocally reinforcing. The more you train yourself to endure insults the stronger you feel psychologically, and therefore the more you can react appropriately and effectively, and vice versa: taking a stance against bullying enables you to see it for the infantile attitude that it really is (even, or especially, when engaged in by "adults"), and this insight then leads to the fostering of greater resilience.

The second caveat stems from an objection I often hear whenever this particular Stoic advice is discussed: perhaps, the argument goes, what you perceive as an insult is only meant as a criticism, even a constructive one. By ignoring it or not taking it seriously, you may miss out on a chance at self-improvement and even come across as arrogant.

In response, we have to remember that one of the four cardinal Stoic virtues is wisdom, the practice of which makes it easier for us to distinguish criticism from insult. Often the distinction is so clear that you don't have to be a Sage to see it. Even so, it is always worth asking yourself a number of questions when you are on the receiving end of what feels like an insult. Is this person a friend or someone you look up to? If yes, then it is more likely that she is just offering advice, perhaps in a somewhat pointed fashion, but with good intentions nonetheless. Even if the person is not likely to be friendly or particularly well positioned to provide you with constructive and useful counsel, perhaps she is seeing something that you don't? In that case too, it is worth ignoring the cutting aspect of what she is saying in order to focus on what it is that she may have gotten right and that may have eluded you. There is no reason at all why insults, even when meant as such, cannot also be teaching moments for us.

10. Don't speak too much about yourself. "In your conversation, don't dwell at excessive length on your own deeds or adventures. Just because you enjoy recounting your exploits doesn't mean that others derive the same pleasure from hearing about them."

I must admit to often failing to follow this advice (see "ego" and "professorial mode" above), but I keep trying. When I do succeed at it, however, not only do I feel good, but I enjoy my social life more. It feels good because, as we have seen with a number of the other exercises—and indeed as the Stoics themselves clearly recognized—there is a peculiar pleasure in being able to exercise some self-control. I can perhaps explain better by making an analogy to going to the gym. I don't know about you, but when I get to my local gym and someone from behind the reception desk smiles and greets me with a loud and cheerful, "Enjoy your workout!" the first thought that comes to my mind is: *Who on earth* enjoys *working out?* Yes, I know, some people actually do enjoy it, but most of us don't. And yet, it is the sort of thing we do because we have reflected on the benefits of doing it and decided that the gain is worth the pain, as they say. But it is also the case that once we get to the end of the workout and head to the shower, we feel a peculiar sort of satisfaction, not only from the physiological benefits of the exercise but also from being able to pat ourselves on the back and say: it was hard, we didn't really want to do it, but we did it!

As for the positive social benefits of this particular spiritual exercise, I think they are obvious: just as no one wants to sit through a slide show from your latest vacation (even when presented as tiny pictures on your latest shining iPhone), no one really wants to hear another person going on and on about himself. It is pretty safe to say that we are not as interesting as we think we are. So trust me (and Epictetus): being a bit more cognizant of that basic truth of social interaction and trying a little harder to take it into account will only make your friends and acquaintances happier.

11. Speak without judging. "Someone bathes in haste; don't say he bathes badly, but in haste. Someone drinks a lot of wine; don't say he drinks badly, but a lot. Until you know their reasons, how do you know that their actions are vicious? This will save you from perceiving one thing clearly, but then assenting to something different."

I'm still working on this one too, I'm afraid. But again, Epictetus's advice is so useful, and so typically Stoic. The idea is to distinguish between matters of fact—to which we can assent if we find them justified by observation—and judgments, from which we generally ought to abstain, since we usually don't have sufficient information.

As we all know, pretty much every day presents us with countless occasions to practice this exercise. Has a friend of yours let himself go in terms of physical appearance? Try to simply describe the fact to yourself, rather than construct a judgment. Then ask yourself why that might have happened. Did your friend *want* to become less attractive or physically fit? Probably not. What were the deeper causes then? And rather than judging the outcome, can you help him instead of sitting there and criticizing him? Or perhaps a coworker has snapped at you, or at someone else. Rather than hurling (or mumbling to yourself) what you think might be an "appropriate" epithet, ask yourself: Have *I* ever snapped at anyone? Yes of course. And when I did so, was it really enjoyable to treat someone like crap? Or were there deeper and not very obvious reasons why I snapped against my better judgment? And how would I have liked others to regard my outburst—what would I have wanted them to do about it? Now make an effort to reverse the situation and see if you can practice Epictetus's advice in the presence of your irritable coworker.

Just pause for a moment and try to imagine how much better the world would be if we all refrained from hasty judgments and looked at human affairs matter-of-factly, with a bit more compassion for our fellow human beings.

12. **Reflect on your day.** "Admit not sleep into your tender eyelids till you have reckoned up each deed of the day—How have I erred, what done or left undone? So start, and so review your acts, and then for vile deeds chide yourself, for good be glad."

This last exercise comes from the *Discourses*, not the *Enchiridion* (and in fact, we have already encountered it), but I think it is crucial and include it here because I have found it extremely beneficial myself. Seneca advises us to do something very similar, and he specifically says that it is best to do it in the evening but before going to bed, because when we are already in bed we tend to become groggy and lose concentration. Find a quiet place in your house or apartment (I can manage that even in the minimalist spaces most people can afford in New York!) and reflect on what has happened during the day. I find it useful to write down my reflections, as Marcus Aurelius did with his "meditations."

The goal is to focus on the important happenings of the day, particularly those that have ethical valence. Perhaps I had a bruising interaction with a colleague today, or didn't treat my partner as well as I should have. Then again, maybe I was magnanimous to a student, or helpful to a friend. For each of these types of occurrences, I write a couple of lines in my philosophical diary, add as dispassionate a comment as I can muster—as if I were grading my own ethical performance that day—and make a mental note of what I have learned from my experiences. On this point I honestly can do no better than to give you a small taste of Seneca himself, arguably the most compelling and elegant of the Stoic writers:

> The spirit ought to be brought up for examination daily. It was the custom of Sextius when the day was over, and he had betaken himself to rest, to inquire of his spirit: "What bad habit of yours have you cured to-day? What vice have you checked? In what respect are you better?" Anger will cease, and become more gentle, if it knows that every day it will have to appear before the judgment seat. What can be more admirable than this fashion of discussing the whole of the day's events? How sweet is the sleep which follows this self-examination? How calm, how sound, and careless is it when our spirit has either received praise or reprimand, and when our secret inquisitor and censor has made his report about our morals? I make use of this privilege, and daily plead my cause before myself: when the lamp is taken out of my sight, and my wife, who knows my habit, has ceased to talk, I pass the whole day in review before myself, and repeat all that I have said and done: I conceal nothing from myself, and omit nothing: for why

should I be afraid of any of my shortcomings, when it is in my power to say, "I pardon you this time: see that you never do that anymore"? . . . A good man delights in receiving advice: all the worst men are the most impatient of guidance.

The Hellenistic Schools of Practical Philosophy

Wonder is the feeling of a philosopher, and philosophy begins in wonder.

—Plato, *Theaetetus*, 155

Throughout this book we have talked about ethics, specifically from the point of view of the Stoics. Ethics, of course, is one of the classical branches of philosophy, the other ones being aesthetics (concerned with beauty and art), epistemology (the study of how we know things), logic (dedicated to understanding reason), and metaphysics (to comprehend the nature of the world).

But as we saw at the beginning of the book, "ethics" has a different meaning today than it did for the ancient Greco-Romans, and of course the Stoics' wasn't the only approach to its study. While modern ethics is essentially concerned with which actions are right or wrong, premodern philosophers conceived of ethics as the much broader inquiry into how to live a happy life, the pursuit of which they deemed to be a human being's most important endeavor. But a happy life can be pursued in different ways, depending on which concept of *eudaimonia*—the flourishing life—one adopts. The major Hellenistic schools of philosophy differed primarily on just this point, and it is useful to get a sense of what the alternatives to Stoicism were—and still are. After all, together with *A Guide to the Good Life*'s author Bill Irvine, I believe that adopting and adapting a philosophy of life to guide you is more important than whichever specific philosophy you end up choosing.

True, there are some pretty awful "philosophies" out there that are not conducive to human flourishing. But there are also several alternatives that may make more sense to you personally—I don't want to leave you with the incorrect impression that it's Stoicism or bust! I will not discuss the variety of life philosophies that arose within the Eastern tradition—Buddhism, Taoism, Confucianism, and the like—because I simply don't know enough about them, and because there are already plenty of excellent resources out there that the interested reader can make use of. Here it will be instructive to take a quick look at those that came out of the Western tradition in the Hellenistic period, before the rise of Christianity. What follows is a simplified genealogical tree of the major Hellenistic schools that either focused on or had a lot to say about the good life.

As you can see, it all began with Socrates. Stemming from different interpretations of his teachings, a trio of schools arose: Plato's Academy, Aristippus's Cyrenaics, and Antisthenes's Cynicism. Aristotelianism originated from within the Academy (which Aristotle frequented), Cyrenaism led to Epicureanism, and Cynicism birthed Stoicism—although the actual relationships among all these schools are best thought

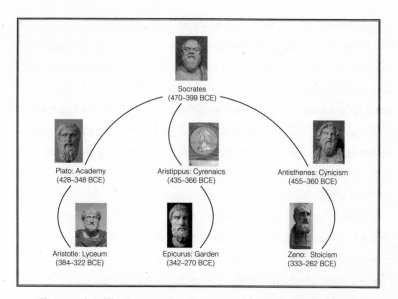

FIGURE A.1. The historical and conceptual relationships among the main Hellenistic schools of philosophy and how they diverged from the thinking of Socrates. *Source*: After Figure 1 in Gordon, "Modern Morality and Ancient Ethics," *Internet Encyclopedia of Philosophy*.

of as many-to-many rather than in terms of linear descent, given the reciprocal influences that took place over centuries. Let's take a brief look at each—who knows, it may turn out that after having learned this much about Stoicism you are really a Cynic or, Zeus forbid, an Epicurean!

Socraticism: We know what Socrates taught mostly (though not exclusively) from the early Platonic dialogues (for example, *Laches, Charmides,* and *Protagoras*). His was the prototype of the ethical approaches to virtue in which wisdom is the Chief Good, the only thing that is always good because it is necessary to make proper use of everything else. For Socrates, our moral imperative is to examine our life, and reason is our best guide in doing so. The eudaimonic life, according to him, consists in acting in the right way, and evil is the result of ignorance, or *amathia* (in other words, nobody purposefully wants to do bad things).

Platonism (the Academy): Plato, in the later dialogues, maintained crucial aspects of Socrates's view (critically, that the eudaimonic life is one of practicing virtue), while at the same time adding a number of metaphysical notions and recasting things in terms of his famous theory of Forms, where the abstract and idealized Form of the Good is the transcendent principle of all goodness. He eventually subordinated individual flourishing to societal needs, as in the Republic, where the ideal state reflects the tripartite division of the human soul, and philosophers, naturally, are in charge of it— just as reason is in charge of the "spirited" and "appetitive" parts of the individual soul.

Aristotelianism (the Peripatetic school, the Lyceum): For Aristotle too, the point of life was to achieve eudaimonia through the practice of the virtues (of which he identified a whopping twelve). In Aristotle's view, there is a proper function for everything in the world, including humans: our proper function is to use reason, so using reason well is the way to live a eudaimonic life. However, we also need some external goods, such as a supportive family and societal environment, some degree of education, health, and wealth, and even some good looks. Crucially, then, being able to live a eudaimonic life is not entirely within the grasp of the agent: some luck, in the form of favorable circumstances, is also needed.

Cyrenaism: Aristippus of Cyrene was, tellingly enough, the first of Socrates's disciples to actually take money for his services. For him, the primary purpose of life was not long-term happiness but rather the moment-to-moment experience of bodily pleasures. To achieve this, one needs practical virtue, but only instrumentally, in order to seek pleasure. Still, we shouldn't think of the Cyrenaics as simply being into sex, drugs, and rock 'n' roll, but rather as seeking what might be called enlightened hedonism. As Aristippus put it: "I possess, but I am not possessed." Self-control was important in order to maintain cheerfulness while making the best of every situation.

Epicureanism (the Garden): Epicurus too taught that life is about increasing one's pleasure and (especially) reducing one's pain. But Epicurean hedonism was much more sophisticated than its Cyrenaic counterpart (despite later Christian smearing, deployed in a successful attempt to fight a threatening rival sect). For one thing, it included mental pleasures, which were considered superior to bodily ones, and happiness was not just a moment-by-moment thing but a lifelong process. The Epicurean way included freeing oneself from prejudice (especially of a religious nature), mastering one's desires, living a modest life, and cultivating friendship. Crucially, however, Epicureans counseled withdrawal from social and political life (because it was much more likely to bring about pain than pleasure).

Cynicism: According to Antisthenes of Athens, the founder of the Cynic school, virtue understood as practical wisdom is not only necessary for a eudaimonic life but also sufficient. That is why the Cynics took the already rather frugal Socratic lifestyle to an extreme. Think of Diogenes of Sinope, Antisthenes's student, who famously lived in a tub, begged for a living, and flaunted just about any social convention. Many Stoics admired the Cynics, and our friend Epictetus devoted the long chapter 22 of the third book of his *Discourses* to an encomium of Cynicism. As he put it, if you really can't be a Cynic, at least be a Stoic.

Stoicism: Zeno of Citium, the founder of Stoicism, learned his philosophy initially from Crates, who was a Cynic and disciple of Diogenes of Sinope. As the reader by now knows well, Stoicism struck a middle ground between Aristotelianism and Cynicism, while at the same time strongly rejecting Epicureanism. The Stoics granted to the Cynics that virtue is both necessary and sufficient for happiness, but also nodded toward the Peripatetics in recovering (some) interest in external goods, which they classified into preferred and dispreferred indifferents, to be pursued, or avoided, so long as they do not compromise one's integrity of character.

All in all, there was a nice conceptual progression and ramification from the Socratic starting point: the Platonic/Aristotelian branch stuck close to Socratic eudaimonism, but the Platonists went mystical (the theory of Forms, the ideal Republic), while the Aristotelians turned pragmatic (some external goods are necessary to achieve eudaimonia). The Cyrenaic/Epicurean branch abandoned the centrality of virtue and turned toward the pleasure-pain dichotomy instead, with the crucial difference that the Cyrenaics considered only bodily moment-to-moment pleasures, while the Epicureans most valued intellectual and lifelong pleasures. (Echoes of their philosophy can be heard in John Stuart Mill and modern utilitarian ethics.) Finally, the Cynic/Stoic branch stuck with the Socratic primacy of virtue, with the Cynics turning

to an ascetic lifestyle and the Stoics elaborating a way to recover (and yet put into perspective) what most people would
consider desirable externals. Both of these schools were highly
influential throughout the history of Christianity.

ACKNOWLEDGMENTS

THIS BOOK IS THE RESULT OF A PERSONAL SPIRITUAL, PHILO-sophical, and intellectual journey that began many years ago and has taken many twists and turns. And I'm sure this won't be the end point either. Many people have directly or indirectly contributed to my journey, and I would like to acknowledge a few of them: Enrica Chiaromonte, my high school philosophy teacher, who instilled in me a passion for the subject that took a quarter-century to finally blossom; Melissa Brenneman, for her support when I made the crazy decision to change careers and become a philosopher; Corinna Colatore, for being there since the beginning of my journey into Stoicism and bearing with my daily practice, no matter how inconvenient it may become at times; my colleagues at the City College of New York, for their support of my idiosyncratic approach to our discipline; the many people behind Stoic Week and STOICON, through whom I discovered Stoicism, and who have welcomed and helped me throughout; my fellow Stoic (and Buddhist) Greg Lopez, who has taught me much about Epictetus, Marcus, and Seneca; Tisse Takagi, my agent, who has been enthusiastic about this project since the beginning and an invaluable guide throughout;

T. J. Kelleher, my editor at Basic Books, whose professionalism keeps striking me every time we work together; and my very careful copyeditor, Cindy Buck.

NOTES

CHAPTER 1: THE UNSTRAIGHTFORWARD PATH

5 **"At this point you run the risk":** Epictetus, *Discourses*, II.12. The full text of Epictetus's *Discourses* is at: http://classics.mit .edu/Epictetus/discourses.html; his shorter *Enchiridion* (or *Handbook*), written in 135 CE and translated by Elizabeth Carter, can be found at: http://classics.mit.edu/Epictetus /epicench.html.

6 **"Death is necessary":** Epictetus, *Discourses*, I.27.

7 **"We die every day":** Seneca, "Letter 24: On Despising Death," in Seneca the Younger, *Complete Works* (Delphi Classics, 2014), 19.

7 **"A man cannot live well":** Seneca, "On Tranquility of Mind," 11.

7 **Every fall thousands of people:** For more information on Stoic Week ("Live Like a Stoic Philosopher for a Week"), see the website at http://modernstoicism.com/. For information on STOICON, the related annual conference of people interested in Stoicism, see http://modernstoicism.com/stoicon -media/.

8 **"no individual":** Quoted in Robert Epstein, "The Prince of Reason," *Psychology Today*, January 1, 2001.

9 **"The philosophical origins":** Aaron T. Beck, A. John Rush, Brian F. Shaw, and Gary Emery, *Cognitive Therapy of Depression* (New York: Guilford Press, 1987), 8.

11 **the clear dichotomy the Stoics drew:** William Irvine, *A Guide to the Good Life* (New York: Oxford University Press, 2008).

11 **this knowledge reinforces the idea:** To clarify what I mean with an example, cognitive scientists have also demonstrated time and again that human beings are bad at estimating probabilities, a fact notoriously exploited by the gambling and lottery industries. But nobody would take those findings as a reason to eliminate the study of statistics; on the contrary, it is precisely such study that can immunize people, at least in part, against common (and sometimes ruinous!) mistakes in quantitative reasoning.

12 **"Men who have made these discoveries":** Seneca, "Letter 33: On the Futility of Learning Maxims," 11.

13 **one of the most renowned teachers in Rome:** Not much remains of Musonius's writings, but they have been collected in an excellent recent translation by Cynthia King, *Musonius Rufus: Lectures and Sayings,* edited and with a preface by William B. Irvine (William B. Irvine, 2011).

14 **arguably the most famous Stoic of all time:** Marcus's *Meditations,* a philosophical diary of personal reflection not originally meant for publication, is one of the most popular books of all time. Like Epictetus's *Discourses,* it has been continuously in print. For a full version, see *The Meditations* by Marcus Aurelius, written in 167 CE and translated by George Long, available at: http://classics.mit.edu/Antoninus/meditations.html.

CHAPTER 2: A ROAD MAP FOR THE JOURNEY

18 **shipwrecked on a voyage:** Diogenes Laertius, *Lives of the Eminent Philosophers,* VII.2, available at: https://en.wiki source.org/wiki/Lives_of_the_Eminent_Philosophers.

19 **who was a long-distance runner:** Both physical jobs and practicing sports often figure in ancient Greco-Roman philosophy. Cleanthes, the second head of the Stoa, was a pugilist and made a living drawing water from gardens.

19 **"but for Chrysippus":** Diogenes Laertius, *Lives of the Eminent Philosophers*, VII.183.

19 **in 155 BCE something very important:** See David Sedley, "The School, from Zeno to Arius Didymus," in *The Cambridge Companion to the Stoics*, edited by Brad Inwood (Cambridge: Cambridge University Press, 2003).

23 **"There are three departments":** Epictetus, *Discourses*, III.2.

24 **Figure 2.1:** This diagram is my own interpretation of a commentary by Donald Robertson (in his *Stoicism and the Art of Happiness: Ancient Tips for Modern Challenges* [Teach Yourself, 2013]), which is in turn derived from the scholarly work of Pierre Hadot, *The Inner Citadel: The Meditations of Marcus Aurelius* (Cambridge, MA: Harvard University Press, 1998).

CHAPTER 3: SOME THINGS ARE IN OUR POWER, OTHERS ARE NOT

30 **"And they said":** Solomon ibn Gabirol, *A Choice of Pearls* (New York: Bloch Publishing Co., 1925), chap. 17, verse 2.

30 **"If there's a remedy":** *The Way of the Bodhisattva* (Boulder, CO: Shambhala Publications, 2008), chap. 6, verse 10.

31 **"Make the best use":** Epictetus, *Enchiridion*, I.1.

33 **"We act very much as if":** Epictetus, *Discourses*, II.5, I.1.

35 **Cicero explains that the archer:** Cicero, *De Finibus Bonorum et Malorum* (About the Ends of Goods and Evils), III.22, in *Complete Works of Cicero* (Delphi Ancient Classics, 2014).

39 **"News was brought him":** Epictetus, *Discourses*, I.1.

40 **"What then is the proper training":** Ibid., III.24.

CHAPTER 4: LIVING ACCORDING TO NATURE

47 **"It is no ordinary task":** Epictetus, *Discourses,* II.9.

51 **We are not the only animals:** Frans de Waal, *Primates and Philosophers: How Morality Evolved* (Princeton, NJ: Princeton University Press, 2009).

51 **the largest brain-to-body ratio:** On the lack of a bone in the human penis and other oddities, see Robert D. Martin, "The Evolution of Human Reproduction: A Primatological Perspective," supplement, *American Journal of Physical Anthropology* 134, no. S45 (2007): 59–84.

51 **what exactly constitutes a language:** On the uniqueness of human language and related topics, see Chet C. Sherwood, Francys Subiaul, and Tadeusz W. Zawidzki, "A Natural History of the Human Mind: Tracing Evolutionary Changes in Brain and Cognition," *Journal of Anatomy* 212 (2008): 426–454.

53 **Some of these shared traits:** A complete list of human universals (always subject to debate and refinement, of course) is found in Donald Brown, *Human Universals* (Philadelphia: Temple University Press, 1991).

54 **"See that you do not act like a sheep":** Epictetus, *Discourses,* II.9.

55 **"In every system of morality":** David Hume, *A Treatise of Human Nature* (London: John Noon, 1739), 335.

56 **ethics has to come from somewhere:** Even today most people still think that the obvious source of morality is a god, but that proposition—which is of course distinct from the question of whether or not a god (or gods) exist—was decidedly refuted 2,400 years ago by none other than Socrates, a big influence on the Stoics. See, for instance, chapter 18 of my *Answers for Aristotle: How Science and Philosophy Can Lead Us to a More Meaningful Life* (New York: Basic Books, 2013).

56 **known as a category mistake:** The concept of a category mistake may perhaps best be understood with the classic example

given in intro philosophy classes: If you ask, "What is the color of triangles?" it may seem that you are asking a deep question, but in fact you are applying a category (color) to a concept (triangles) that the category simply does not belong to. Triangles, as abstract geometrical figures, are described in terms of angles, sizes, and so forth, but not in terms of color—although of course a *particular* triangle may have a certain color. Still, you may fool someone for a few seconds at a cocktail party with that sort of question. Just make sure to quickly move away before your interlocutor has had time to think about it for a few seconds.

57 **we do indeed have a moral instinct:** For an accessible piece on the concept of the moral instinct, see Stephen Pinker, "The Moral Instinct," *New York Times Magazine,* January 13, 2008.

58 **as we approach the age of reason:** The so-called five- to seven-year shift (or six- to eight-), intuited by the ancients, is now a well-established scientific concept, backed by solid evidence from both psychology and neuroscience. See, for instance, Arnold J. Sameroff and Marshall M. Haith, *The Five to Seven Year Shift: The Age of Reason and Responsibility* (Chicago: University of Chicago Press, 1996).

58 **"the nature of the rational animal":** Epictetus, *Discourses,* I.19.

59 **"Each of us is, as it were":** *Ethical Fragments of Hierocles, Preserved by Stobaeus,* translated by Thomas Taylor (1822). See the fragment "How we ought to conduct ourselves towards our kindred."

61 **"Never . . . reply to one":** Epictetus, *Discourses,* I.9.

CHAPTER 5: PLAYING BALL WITH SOCRATES

64 **"[Socrates] was like one playing":** Epictetus, *Discourses,* II.5.

65 **Greco-Roman soccer:** There is pretty good evidence that both the Greeks and the Romans played some kind of soccer, though

the rules of the game have not survived. The National Museum of Archaeology in Athens houses a marble relief featuring an adult and a child, with the adult clearly balancing what the Romans called a *folis*, which looks like a soccer ball (that is, an inflated ball). Moreover, Ulpiano tells of a court case in Rome over a man who was getting a shave in a barber shop being killed by a flying soccer ball of the *pile* type, which was characterized by stitches very much like those of modern soccer balls. See Digesto, IX, 2, 11, pr. 1.

65 **making the obstacle the way:** "Our actions may be impeded by [others], but there can be no impeding our intentions or our dispositions. Because we can accommodate and adapt. The mind adapts and converts to its own purposes the obstacle to our acting. The impediment to action advances action. What stands in the way becomes the way." Marcus Aurelius, *Meditations*, V.20.

66 **"How do I know what is going":** Epictetus, *Discourses*, II.5.

69 **"I was imbued with":** Seneca, *Epistles*, 108, 22.

70 **"although there are many pleasures":** Musonius Rufus, "The Lecture About Food," *Lectures*, part B, 3, 7, and 8, in Musonius Rufus, *Lectures and Sayings*, translated by Cynthia King (CreateSpace, 2011).

71 **there really are only two options:** Many so-called informal logical fallacies are actually not fallacious at all, or at least not always. Often they are simple heuristics—shortcuts one can use in a pinch to arrive at a satisfactory understanding of a situation, or a preliminary judgment. Hurling accusations of logical fallacies is a particularly common practice in discussions of pseudoscientific claims, as my colleagues and I have argued in this paper: Maarten Boudry, Fabio Paglieri, and Massimo Pigliucci, "The Fake, the Flimsy, and the Fallacious: Demarcating Arguments in Real Life," *Argumentation* 29 (2015): 431–456.

71 **Eleven Madison Park:** Curious about why I picked on Eleven Madison Park? Because of this article (Edward Frame, "Dinner and Deception," *New York Times,* August 22, 2015) by one of their former "captains," which provides a behind-the-scenes look at the culture of service there and the customers who use it and abuse it. I should add that I very much doubt that Eleven Madison Park is special in this respect.

72 **"If [you] must live in a palace":** Marcus Aurelius, *Meditations,* V.16.

74 **Diogenes seriously practiced:** Much of what we know of the life and adventures of Diogenes the Cynic comes from another Diogenes, Laertius, in his *Lives and Opinions of Eminent Philosophers.*

75 **"great difference between joy and pain":** Seneca, *On Various Aspects of Virtue,* 18.

75 **the concept of lexicographic preferences:** I must thank one of the readers of my howtobeastoic.org blog, who goes by the handle "timbartik," for pointing me in the direction of lexicographic ordering as a good model of the distinction between virtue and preferred indifferents.

76 **standard economic theory simply does not apply:** A number of philosophers have implicitly used lexicographic ordering when making the case that a particular good should not be for sale; see, for instance, Michael J. Sandel, *What Money Can't Buy: The Moral Limits of Markets* (New York: Farrar, Straus & Giroux, 2012), and Debra Satz, *Why Some Things Should Not Be for Sale: The Moral Limits of Markets* (New York: Oxford University Press, 2010).

CHAPTER 6: GOD OR ATOMS??

79 **"Who is it that has fitted the sword":** Epictetus, *Discourses,* I.6.

80 **such as Thomas Aquinas:** Thomas Aquinas, *Summa Theologiae* (1273), Article 3, Question 2.

80 **"In crossing a heath":** William Paley, *Natural Theology: or, Evidence of the Existence and Attributes of the Deity, Collected from the Appearance of Nature* (London: J. Faulder, 1802), ch. 1.

81 **"If we see a house":** David Hume, *Dialogues Concerning Natural Religion* (1779), part II.

83 **"But I own that I cannot see":** Charles Darwin (1903), *More Letters of Charles Darwin*, edited by Francis Darwin and A. C. Seward (New York: D. Appleton and Co., 1903), 252. See also Sara Joan Miles, "Charles Darwin and Asa Gray Discuss Teleology and Design," *Perspectives on Science and Christian Faith* 53 (September 2001): 196–201, available at: http://goo.gl/kbdNR5.

83 **"Slave, do you mean to arraign":** Epictetus, *Discourses*, I.12. A position very close to Epictetus's has recently been articulated and defended with modern arguments by the philosopher Tim Mulgan in his *Purpose in the Universe: The Moral and Metaphysical Case for Ananthropocentric Purposivism* (New York: Oxford University Press, 2015).

84 **"You are a principal work":** Epictetus, *Discourses*, II.8.

84 **or perhaps panentheistic:** There is a subtle but important distinction between pantheism and panentheism: in the first case, God is identical to Nature; in the second, God interpenetrates Nature (that is, God is everywhere), but there is a distinction between God and Nature nonetheless. What makes the Stoic case a bit difficult to decide is that, on the one hand, they used the terms "God" (or "Zeus," but not referring to the Olympian version) and "Nature" interchangeably. But they also believed that the universe is made of matter, some of which (all living beings, including humans) also partakes of the rational principle, the Logos. So their metaphysics really

had elements of both pantheism and panentheism—not that it really matters for my purposes here.

85 **"Concerning the gods"**: Epictetus, *Discourses*, I.12. For "where'er I move / Thou seest me," see Homer, *Iliad*, X.279.

87 **"That which is true is mine"**: Seneca, *Epistles*, I.12.11.

87 **"To the gods I am indebted"**: Marcus Aurelius, *Meditations*, I.17.

87 **"Since it is possible"**: Ibid., II.11.

88 **"You have embarked"**: Ibid., III.3.

88 **"Either there is a fatal necessity"**: Ibid., XII.14.

88 **even before New Atheism**: For my, shall we say, more mature take on the New Atheism, see: "New Atheism and the Scientistic Turn in the Atheism Movement," *Midwest Studies in Philosophy* 37, no. 1 (2015): 142–153, available at: http://philpapers .org/rec/PIGNAA.

88 **When I was living in Tennessee**: For a taste of my debates, if you are so inclined, see "Dr. Massimo Pigliucci vs. Kent Hovind [a creationist]," posted March 7, 2012, https://goo .gl/oab5OX; "William Lane Craig [a theologian] vs. Massimo Pigliucci," posted December 9, 2012, https://goo.gl/D4T7h7; and "Creation/Evolution Debate: Dr. [Duane] Gish [a creationist] vs. Dr. [Massimo] Pigliucci, May 20, 1999, Part 1," posted April 6, 2013, https://goo.gl/txfKjG.

91 **"There are many questions in philosophy"**: Cicero, *The Nature of the Gods*, in *Complete Works of Cicero* (Delphi Ancient Classics, 2014).

CHAPTER 7: IT'S ALL ABOUT CHARACTER (AND VIRTUE)

95 **"When Vespasian sent to him"**: Epictetus, *Discourses*, I.2.

98 **the only human ability**: A thorough discussion of Socrates's take on wisdom as the chief good is found in the Platonic dialogue known as the *Euthydemus*. Plato, *Euthydemus*,

translated by G. A. McBryer and M. P. Nichols, introduction by D. Schaeffer (Focus Philosophical Library, 2010). I published a commentary on it from a Stoic perspective, "Why Plato's *Euthydemus* Is Relevant to Stoics," How to Be a Stoic, August 20, 2015, available at: https://goo.gl/9K3t2a.

99 **we must have wisdom:** The ancients recognized two types of wisdom: *sophia*, which refers to the ability to understand the nature of the world—the word "philosophy" means "love" (*philo*) of "wisdom" (*sophos*)—and *phronêsis*, or practical wisdom, the ability to make good decisions in your life, and one of the four Stoic virtues. Lack of *sophia*, as we will soon see, has its own word, *amathia*, which leads to moral error regardless of your intelligence and education. Being smart and cultured, in other words, is no assurance of being wise.

100 **A study by Katherine Dahlsgaard:** Katherine Dahlsgaard, Christopher Peterson, and Martin E. P. Seligman, "Shared Virtue: The Convergence of Valued Human Strengths Across Culture and History," *Review of General Psychology* 9 (2005): 203–213.

100 **six "core" virtues:** The list is adapted from ibid., table 1.

102 **"The Pythagoreans bid us":** Marcus Aurelius, *Meditations*, XI.27.

103 **"Lay aside the senator's dress'":** Epictetus, *Discourses*, I.29.

104 **"You are a man":** Ibid., II.3.

106 **"For the helmsman to wreck his vessel":** Ibid., IV.3.

CHAPTER 8: A VERY CRUCIAL WORD

110 **"Manifold are thy shapings":** Quoted in *Robert Browning: Selected Poems*, edited by John Woolford, Daniel Karlin, and Joseph Phelan (New York: Routledge, 2013), 364.

111 **"This is the defense":** Epictetus, *Discourses*, I.26.

111 **"What is the reason":** Ibid., I.28.

112 **"During the war, Ernst Jünger":** Thanks to my friend Amy Valladares for pointing out this interview to me and for

translating the bit I quote here. The full interview, "Hannah Arendt im Gespräch mit Joachim Fest (1964)" (in German), can be found at: https://goo.gl/JOeyJC (posted August 8, 2014). An English-language transcript was published as *Hannah Arendt: The Last Interview and Other Conversations* (New York: Melville House, 2013).

114 **"Wisdom alone":** Plato, *Euthydemus,* 281d.

114 **Belangia has written extensively:** Sherwood Belangia, "Ignorance vs. Stupidity," Shared Ignorance, September 8, 2014, https://goo.gl/vmIohg.

114 **an Athenian general and politician:** Alcibiades is a wonderfully interesting historical figure about whom—surprisingly—nobody seems to have written a biography or made a movie. They ought to. He began the Peloponnesian War on the side of Athens, his native city. He was eventually exiled and defected to Sparta, for whom he engineered a number of defeats of Athens. Then he became unpopular in Sparta as well, so he defected to Persia, the sworn enemy of the Greek city-states. He was then recalled by Athens, where he engineered what turned out to be the disastrous invasion of Sicily, arguably a major reason why Athens eventually lost the war. But it could have gone otherwise had Alcibiades actually been able to lead the expedition as planned. Instead, his fellow citizens exiled him again and gave command to the inept Nicias. Alcibiades then fled once more, this time to Phrygia, where he sought help to fight Sparta. He was probably killed by Spartan agents in the mountains of Phrygia.

114 **"But if you are bewildered":** *Alcibiades Major,* 118a–c, in *Plato in Twelve Volumes,* vol. 8, translated by W. R. M. Lamb (Cambridge, MA: Harvard University Press; London: William Heinemann Ltd., 1955).

116 **"A-gnoia means literally":** Belangia, "Ignorance vs. Stupidity," available at: https://woodybelangia.com/2014/09/08/ignorance-vs-stupidity/.

116 **elucidation of the concept of** *amathia:* Glenn Hughes quoted in ibid. from an essay entitled "Voegelin's Use of Musil's Concept of Intelligent Stupidity in Hitler and the Germans" (Eric Voegelin Institute, 2007).

117 **"I know full well":** Euripides, *Medea*, 1078.

117 **"Here the very gratification":** Epictetus, *Discourses*, I.28.

118 **"Every error implies conflict":** Ibid., II.26.

120 **the more clever people are:** Michael Shermer, *Why People Believe Weird Things* (San Francisco: W. H. Freeman, 1997).

120 **help students change their conceptual outlook:** Barbara J. Guzzetti, Tonja E. Snyder, Gene V. Glass, and Warren S. Gamas, "Promoting Conceptual Change in Science: A Comparative Meta-analysis of Instructional Interventions from Reading Education and Science Education," *Reading Research Quarterly* 28 (1993): 116–159.

120 **"'Such a one reviled you'":** Epictetus, *Discourses*, IV.5.

CHAPTER 9: THE ROLE OF ROLE MODELS

125 **"Oh, that's easy":** Stephen Palmer, "The Stockdale Paradox: The Right Way to Leverage Hope," http://stephendpalmer .com/stockdale-paradox-hope/.

126 **Stockdale became a fellow:** Two essays by Stockdale on Stoicism are available online: "The Stoic Warrior Triad: Tranquility, Fearlessness, and Freedom," lecture delivered April 18, 1995, http://goo.gl/dszFyQ; and "Master of My Fate: A Stoic Philosopher in a Hanoi Prison," n.d., http://goo.gl/jrooWm.

126 **"After ejection":** VADM James B. Stockdale, "Stockdale on Stoicism II: Master of My Fate," 5, https://www.usna.edu /Ethics/_files/documents/Stoicism2.pdf.

127 **"By the time the tackling":** VADM James B. Stockdale, "Stockdale on Stoicism I: The Stoic Warrior's Triad," 16, https://www.usna.edu/Ethics/_files/documents/stoicism1.pdf.

127 **"Lameness is an impediment":** Epictetus, *Enchiridion*, 9.

128 **"When a man who has set his will":** Epictetus, *Discourses,* IV.7.

128 **Lieutenants Clark Kent and Ben Casey:** Clark Kent is, of course, Superman's alter ego. Ben Casey was the surgeon protagonist of *Ben Casey,* a popular American television series of the early 1960s.

129 **"Tranquillity, fearlessness":** Epictetus, *Discourses,* III.15.

130 **modern biology and developmental psychology:** See Massimo Pigliucci, *Phenotypic Plasticity: Beyond Nature and Nurture* (Baltimore: Johns Hopkins University Press, 2001).

130 **"Can you tell me, Socrates":** The following discussion is informed by a clear and compelling paper by Hugh Mercer Cutler, "Can Virtue Be Taught?" *Humanitas* 7, no. 1 (1994), http://www.nhinet.org/humsub/curtl7–1.pdf.

131 **Kohlberg's theory has been criticized:** See Lawrence Kohlberg, Charles Levine, and Alexandra Hewer, *Moral Stages: A Current Formulation and a Response to Critics* (Basel: Karger Publishing, 1983).

132 **a major aspect of the environment:** Pigliucci, *Phenotypic Plasticity,* 253–262.

133 **the nature of the wise person:** Seneca, "On the Firmness of the Wise Person," in *Complete Works.*

134 **known as Cato the Younger:** For a recent biography of Cato, see Rob Goodman and Jimmy Soni, *Rome's Last Citizen: The Life and Legacy of Cato, Mortal Enemy of Caesar* (New York: St. Martin's Press/Thomas Dunne Books, 2012).

135 **"Cato did not immediately die":** Plutarch, "Life of Cato," in *Parallel Lives,* Delphi Complete Works of Plutarch (Delphi Classics, 2013), 70.6.

136 **"What about ordinary life":** Massimo Pigliucci, "On Death and Stoicism," IN SIGHT series, Aeon, https://aeon.co/videos/how-the-stoic-embrace-of-death-can-help-us-get-a-grip-on-life.

CHAPTER 10: DISABILITY AND MENTAL ILLNESS

140 **Becker, now a retired professor:** Lawrence Becker, *A New Stoicism* (Princeton, NJ: Princeton University Press, 1997).

140 **I spent several months discussing:** The New York City Stoics meet-up group can be found at: http://www.meetup.com /New-York-City-Stoics/.

140 **the two of us were introduced:** One of the outcomes of meeting Larry Becker was an interview that I did with him on different aspects of Stoic theory and practice. "Interview with Larry Becker" was posted in four parts on March 22, 24, 29, and 31, 2016, on the How to Be a Stoic website: https://goo .gl/cfPGgL; https://goo.gl/FyFZT8; https://goo.gl/hKgW1w; and https://goo.gl/Gcc6La.

140 **video . . . for Post-Polio Health International:** The video of Larry Becker's address at a meeting of the Post-Polio Health International, "Developing a Personal Philosophy About Disability," is available at: http://www.polioplace.org /personal-philosophy-disability.

144 **modern cognitive science clearly shows:** For a few examples of studies showing that "consumer paralysis" results from having too many choices, see Hazel Rose Markus and Barry Schwartz, "Does Choice Mean Freedom and Well-being?" *Journal of Consumer Research* 37 (2010): 344–355; Tina Harrison, Kathryn Waite, and Phil White, "Analysis by Paralysis: The Pension Purchase Decision Process," *International Journal of Bank Marketing* 24 (2006): 5–23; and Graeme Drummond, "Consumer Confusion: Reduction Strategies in Higher Education," *International Journal of Educational Management* 18 (2006): 317–323.

146 **"Bear and forbear":** Epictetus, Aulus Gellius, *Noctes Acticae*, xii.19.

147 **Our acquaintance:** See Andrew Overby, "How Stoicism Helped Me Overcome Depression," Stoicism Today, September 19, 2015, http://goo.gl/sIGWuR.

147 **what it is like to be another person:** As it turns out, "what is it like to be [not you]" is one of those impossible philosophical problems; see Thomas Nagel, "What Is It Like to Be a Bat?" *Philosophical Review* 83, no. 4 (October 1974): 435–450, http://goo.gl/PjZSeM.

149 **"The art of life":** Marcus Aurelius, *Meditations*, VII.61.

150 **"One of the most interesting developments":** William Irvine, *A Guide to the Good Life: The Ancient Art of Stoic Joy* (New York: Oxford University Press, 2008), 254.

151 **"Stand by a stone":** Epictetus, *Discourses*, I.25.

152 **I don't even know the name:** See "Stoicism as a Means to Cope with Autism," Stoicism Today, April 26, 2015, http://goo.gl/YOQBfM. I do not have space here to discuss several more modern Stoics I'm aware of whose approaches to personal, nontrivial problems in life provide additional examples of the power of this philosophy; see Leonidas Konstantakos, "On Epictetus and Post-Traumatic Stress," Stoicism Today, January 30, 2016, http://goo.gl/oxXDrl; Chris Peden, "Autism and Stoicism I," Stoicism Today, April 25, 2015, http://goo.gl/ogXOyV (written from the point of view of a parent of two autistic children); and the powerfully moving essay by Marco Bronx, "In Praise of Chronic Pain: A Stoic Meditation," Stoicism Today, July 30, 2016, https://goo.gl/F5zOi2.

153 **"Our relations with one another":** Seneca, "On the Usefulness of Basic Principles," *Letters to Lucilius,* XCV.53.

153 **"I do not know whether":** Seneca, "On Reformation," *Letters to Lucilius,* XXV.2.

CHAPTER 11: ON DEATH AND SUICIDE

157 **They were aware of death:** Similarly empowering notions of death are found in other philosophies, such as Epicureanism (Stoicism's direct rival) and Buddhism (Stoicism's Eastern cousin).

158 **"Why does an as of wheat grow?":** Epictetus, *Discourses*, II.6.

159 **"Will you realize once for all":** Ibid., III.26.

160 **later figures influenced by Stoicism:** The title of one of Michel de Montaigne's famous essays (collected in a book that gave the name to the entire modern genre) was "That to Study Philosophy Is to Learn to Die" (1580); the full text is available at: https://en.wikisource.org/wiki/The_Essays_of_Montaigne. Tellingly, it begins: "Cicero says 'that to study philosophy is nothing but to prepare one's self to die.'"

160 **"Death, therefore":** Epicurus, "Letter to Menoeceus," http://www.epicurus.net/en/menoeceus.html.

160 **"You shall bear illness well":** Epictetus, *Discourses*, III.26.

161 **"What do you mean":** Ibid., IV.7.

162 **This is not the place to explain:** Should you be curious, I've developed those reasons in detail in Massimo Pigliucci, "Mind Uploading: A Philosophical Counter-analysis," in *Intelligence Unbound: The Future of Uploaded and Machine Minds*, edited by Russell Blackford and Damien Broderick (Hoboken, NJ: Wiley, 2014).

163 **"Yes, those at the Mysteries":** Epictetus, *Discourses*, IV.1.

164 **On the weekend of July 23 and 24, 2016:** Julie Watson, "Terminally Ill Woman Holds Party Before Ending Her Life," Associated Press, August 11, 2016, http://goo.gl/jqOr2A.

164 **"If it is not to your profit":** Epictetus, *Discourses*, II.1.

164 **The "open door":** Interpreting Epictetus's "open door" as a reference to suicide is widely accepted in ancient philosophy scholarship. See, for instance, W. O. Stephens, "Epictetus on Fearing Death: Bugbear and Open Door Policy," *Ancient Philosophy* 34 (2014): 365–391.

164 **"Suppose someone made the room smoke":** Epictetus, *Discourses*, I.25.

166 **"For the foot (for instance)":** Ibid., II.5.

167 **The last example is Seneca:** Two recent biographies of Seneca have somewhat different takes on his moral fiber and philosophical coherence: James Romm, *Dying Every Day: Seneca at the Court of Nero* (New York: Alfred A. Knopf, 2014); and Emily Wilson, *The Greatest Empire: A Life of Seneca* (New York: Oxford University Press, 2014).

169 **"Let me describe another state":** Epictetus, *Discourses,* II.15.

170 **"Stay where you are":** Ibid., I.9.

CHAPTER 12: HOW TO DEAL WITH ANGER, ANXIETY, AND LONELINESS

171 **Aristophanes made fun of Socrates:** Plato did not appreciate Aristophanes's lampooning of his teacher and went so far as to partially blame the playwright, in his dialogue *Phaedo*, for Socrates's later execution by the Athenian state. The claim is doubtful, but not entirely unjustified, according to modern scholars.

172 **"Yesterday I had an iron lamp":** Epictetus, *Discourses,* I.18 and I.29.

173 **But our sage disagrees:** Ironically, Lucian of Samosata tells us that when Epictetus died, a friend of his got hold of a lamp that had belonged to the philosopher and managed to sell it for the excellent price of 3,000 drachmas. I'm pretty sure the philosopher would have disapproved.

174 **modern psychological research:** A useful article on recognizing and managing anger from a modern psychological perspective is: American Psychological Association, "Controlling Anger Before It Controls You," http://www.apa.org/topics /anger/control.aspx.

175 **"'What!' you say":** Epictetus, *Discourses,* I.18.

175 **approaches to reforming criminals:** For three examples of prison systems that a Stoic would endorse, see "Inside

Norway's Progressive Prison System," CNN, August 3, 2011, http://edition.cnn.com/2011/WORLD/europe/08/02/vbs .norwegian.prisons/; "Progressive Prison Keeps Door Open," This Is Finland, http://finland.fi/life-society/progressive -prison-keeps-doors-open/; and "Nicholas Turner and Jeremy Travis, "What We Learned from German Prisons," *New York Times*, August 6, 2015.

175 **the early intuitions of the Stoics:** APA, "Controlling Anger Before It Controls You."

180 **"When I see a man":** Epictetus, *Discourses*, II.12.

181 **Worse things happen at sea:** I hope you know what I'm re-ferring to. If not, take a look at "Monty Python: Always Look on the Bright Side of Life," https://youtu.be/jHPOzQzk9Qo (around 2'30") (uploaded July 28, 2006).

181 **"We are anxious for our bit":** Epictetus, *Discourses*, II.13.

182 **headlines that read:** Here are the pertinent articles: Rebecca Harris, "The Loneliness Epidemic: We're More Connected Than Ever—But Are We Feeling More Alone?" *The Inde-pendent*, March 30, 2015; Vanessa Barford, "Is Modern Life Making Us Lonely?" *BBC News Magazine*, April 8, 2013; and Janice Shaw Crouse, "The Loneliness of American Society," *The American Spectator*, May 18, 2014. A quick Google search will reveal many, many more.

182 **interesting discussion of loneliness:** Colin Killeen, "Lone-liness: An Epidemic in Modern Society," *Journal of Advanced Nursing* 28 (1998): 762–770.

183 **"[Loneliness] is such an innate part":** Ibid., 762.

184 **"The forlorn state is the condition":** Epictetus, *Discourses*, III.13.

CHAPTER 13: LOVE AND FRIENDSHIP

187 **"I am so miserable":** This and the following quotes regarding Epictetus's encounter with the distraught father are from *Dis-courses*, I.11.

190 **"But though we are capable":** Ibid., IV.5.

190 **"We see that the carpenter":** Ibid., II.14 and I.29.

191 *storgē*, **a far less frequently used word:** This sense of the inevitability of *storgē* explains why the word, counterintuitively, was also used to indicate some things we have no choice but to put up with, like "loving" a tyrant.

193 **"For where else is friendship":** Epictetus, *Discourses*, II.22.

Chapter 14: Practical Spiritual Exercises

201 **a number of other recent books:** These very practical books on Stoicism include William B. Irvine, *A Guide to the Good Life: The Ancient Art of Stoic Joy* (New York: Oxford University Press, 2008); and Donald Robertson, *Stoicism and the Art of Happiness: Ancient Tips for Modern Challenges* (Teach Yourself, 2013).

203 **I have gone through the *Enchiridion*:** Many thanks to my friend, fellow Stoic, and collaborator on many ventures, Greg Lopez, who has generously helped me put together these exercises.

203 **The first goal is to become mindful:** Greg and I have put together a broader set of exercises, twenty-four in total, by adding several more to this list from Marcus Aurelius's *Meditations*. For the full package, go to How to Be a Stoic, "Collections," https://howtobeastoic.wordpress.com/collections/.

204 **In modern economic theory:** As discussed in Chapter 5, lexicographic ordering is at work when some philosophers argue that particular goods should not be for sale; see Sandel, *What Money Can't Buy*, and Satz, *Why Some Things Should Not Be for Sale*.

205 **"So make a practice":** Epictetus, *Enchiridion*, I.5.

207 **"Agents are required":** Lawrence C. Becker, *A New Stoicism* (Princeton, NJ: Princeton University Press, 1997), 42.

207 **"In the case of particular things":** Epictetus, *Enchiridion*, III.

211 **"Whenever planning an action"**: Ibid., IV.

214 **"For every challenge"**: Ibid., X.

215 **"bear and forbear"**: Epictetus, *Discourses*, IV.8.

216 **"Remember, it is not enough"**: Epictetus, *Enchiridion*, XX.

217 **"[The next time] you encounter"**: Ibid., CI.

217 **"We can familiarize ourselves"**: Ibid., XXVI.

219 **"Let silence be your goal"**: Ibid., XXXIII.2.

222 **"Avoid fraternizing"**: Ibid., XXXIII.6.

223 **"If you learn that someone"**: Ibid., XXXIII.9.

224 **an active set of social networks:** On Twitter, https://twitter .com/mpigliucci.

225 **two blogs:** My blog on general philosophy can be found at platofootnote.org; the one on Stoicism at howtobeastoic.org.

226 **"In your conversation"**: Epictetus, *Enchiridion*, XXXIII.14.

228 **"Someone bathes in haste"**: Ibid., XLV.

229 **"Admit not sleep"**: Epictetus, Aulus Gellius, *Noctes Acticae*, xii.19.

230 **"The spirit ought to be brought up"**: Seneca, *On Anger*, III.36.

APPENDIX: THE HELLENISTIC SCHOOLS OF PRACTICAL PHILOSOPHY

234 **a simplified genealogical tree:** The diagram is adapted from John-Stewart Gordon, "Modern Morality and Ancient Ethics," Internet Encyclopedia of Philosophy, http://www.iep .utm.edu/anci-mod/ (accessed May 27, 2016).

234 **it all began with Socrates:** There is a reason why the whole history of Western philosophy is divided into pre-Socratics and whatever happened from Socrates onward.

INDEX

263